The Merrill Studies in The House of the Seven Gables

CHARLES E. MERRILL STUDIES
*Under the General Editorship of
Matthew J. Bruccoli and Joseph Katz*

The Merrill Studies in The House of the Seven Gables

Compiled by
Roger Asselineau
The Sorbonne, Paris

Charles E. Merrill Publishing Company
A Bell & Howell Company
Columbus, Ohio

Copyright © 1970 by Charles E. Merrill Publishing Company, Columbus, Ohio. All rights reserved. No part of this book may be reproduced in any form, electronic or mechanical, including photocopy, recording, or any information storage and retrieval system without permission in writing from the publisher.

ISBN: 0-675-09246-9

Library of Congress Catalog Number: 73-146037

1 2 3 4 5 6 7 8 9 10—80 79 78 77 76 75 74 73 72 71

Printed in the United States of America

Preface

When *The House of the Seven Gables* appeared in 1851 close on the heels of *The Scarlet Letter* it was almost universally regarded as superior to its predecessor and hailed as Hawthorne's masterpiece. Such was in particular the unanimous conclusion of the six contemporary critics (French as well as American) whose reviews are reprinted in Part I. Hawthorne himself seems to have thought so, as the letter he wrote to Horatio Bridge conclusively shows. Melville, who was then living a few miles away from him at Lenox, must have caught the infection of this enthusiasm, for he immediately sent an excited letter to his friend in the form of an imaginary review for an imaginary magazine.

This preference will probably seem strange to twentieth century readers. Most of them, without a doubt, instinctively agree with Henry James that *The House of the Seven Gables* is "not so rounded and complete as *The Scarlet Letter*." It does not have the stark grandeur, the pure outlines and stylized beauty of *The Scarlet Letter*. It is diffuse by comparison. *The Scarlet Letter* has the noble ethereality and simplicity of a French classical tragedy. It concentrates with ruthless vigor and rigor on the eternal triangle Hester-Dimmesdale-Chillingworth superimposed on Hawthorne's own metaphysical triangle, Man-God-the Devil, with young Pearl impishly frolicking around. *The House of the Seven Gables* looks overcrowded and overfurnished by comparison, more melodramatic than tragic and yet strangely empty and decidedly too sentimental.

Yet it is unfair to decry *The House of the Seven Gables* by contrasting it with *The Scarlet Letter*. It should be judged independently. It was written in a different key and with a different purpose. There is a difference in kind rather than degree between the two books. With *The House of the Seven Gables* we leave the rarefied atmosphere of seventeenth century Salem; we are back on earth. This is no "roman démeublé," no unfurnished novel (to take up Willa Cather's phrase) like *The Scarlet Letter*; Hawthorne has done his best to furnish it (Melville praised him for it in his letter). His aim was to give us a complete picture of contemporary American life from a quiet elm-shadowed New England street to a noisy railway depot. He has striven hard to fill up the vacuum which was to frighten away Henry James a few decades later. Though he has only partly succeeded in his attempt, he has at least provided a plausible setting for his story of heredity and predestination and social change, a suitable frame for a less austere and more smiling evocation of the American scene.

So there is definitely a case for *The House of the Seven Gables*, and it has been very convincingly argued by a number of critics whose essays constitute the bulky Part III of this anthology. They examine in turn all the aspects of the novel: its historical and metaphysical contents, its psycho-analytical implications (as seriously as if it were *Winnie the Pooh*), its structure and metaphorical patterns. The essay of Francis J. Battaglia fittingly winds up the debate, for it vindicates Hawthorne against the critics who object to the apparent lack of coherence of the plot and to the gratuity and artificiality of the ending. In this "new light" *The House of the Seven Gables* appears more strongly unified both dramatically and thematically than was often thought.

Whatever critics may say, though, readers of Hawthorne will probably always be divided between those who place *The House of the Seven Gables* above all his other works and those who prefer *The Scarlet Letter*. These two extreme positions are represented in Part V by T. S. Eliot and D. H. Lawrence. The former studying "The Hawthorne Aspect of Henry James" naturally preferred the less passionate of Hawthorne's two books and concluded that *The House of the Seven Gables* was "Hawthorne's best novel after all." The latter, on the contrary, contemptuously dismissed it and boldly proclaimed: "Hawthorne's other books are nothing compared to *The Scarlet Letter*."

Preface

In such a quarrel arguments pro and con are of no avail and will sway no one. Each reader's choice will in the last resort be determined by his or her temperament. But this anthology will at least show admirers of *The House of the Seven Gables* that they have no reason for being ashamed of their preference. The book is not so simple as it looks. Each gable has its beauty and its mystery and Alice's Posies are in a way "flowers of evil."

R. A.

Contents

Nathaniel Hawthorne
   A Better Book Than *The Scarlet Letter*   3

Herman Melville
   A Little Criticism from "The Pittsfield Secret Review"   4

Anonymous
   [Exquisite Beauty of Finish]   7

[Rufus W. Griswold]
   The Purest Piece of Imagination in Our Prose Literature   9

[Andrew Preston Peabody]
   [The Most Successful of His Romances]   10

Henry Theodore Tuckerman
   [A Flemish Painting]   13

Anonymous
   [Truthful Delineations of Character]   17

E[mile] D[urand] Forgues
   [A French View]   19

Henry James
   [A Magnificent Fragment]   23

Frederick C. Crews
   [A Psychoanalytical Interpretation]   33

Henry Nash Smith
  [*The House of the Seven Gables* as Social History]   50

Edward C. Sampson
  [Some Sights and Sounds]   56

Klaus Lubbers
  Metaphorical Patterns   60

William B. Dillingham
  Structure and Theme   74

Francis J. Battaglia
  New Light on Old Problems   86

D. H. Lawrence
  "Nothing Compared to *The Scarlet Letter*"   111

T. S. Eliot
  "Hawthorne's Best Novel After All"   113

1. Contemporaneous Reactions
(including the author's)

Nathaniel Hawthorne

A Better Book than "The Scarlet Letter"

Why did you not write and tell me how you liked, or how you did not like, the 'House of the Seven Gables'? Did you feel shy of expressing an unfavorable opinion? It would not have hurt me in the least, though I am always glad to please you; but I rather think I have reached that stage when I do not care, very essentially one way or the other, for anybody's opinion on any one production. On this last romance, for instance, I have heard and seen such diversity of judgment that I should be altogether bewildered if I attempted to strike a balance. So I take nobody's estimate unless it happens to agree with my own. I think it a work more characteristic of my mind, and more proper and natural for me to write, than 'The Scarlet Letter'; but for that very reason, less likely to interest the public. Nevertheless it appears to have sold better than the former, and, I think, is more sure of retaining the ground it acquires. Mrs. Kemble writes that both works are popular in England, and advises me to take out my copyright there.

From Horatio Bridge, *Personal Recollections of Nathaniel Hawthorne* (New York, 1893), pp. 126-127. A letter sent by Hawthorne to Bridge on July 22, 1851.

Herman Melville

A Little Criticism from "The Pittsfield Secret Review"

"The House of the Seven Gables: A Romance. By Nathaniel Hawthorne. One vol. 16mo, pp. 344." The contents of this book do not belie its rich, clustering, romantic title. With great enjoyment we spent almost an hour in each separate gable. This book is like a fine old chamber, abundantly, but still judiciously, furnished with precisely that sort of furniture best fitted to furnish it. There are rich hangings, wherein are braided scenes from tragedies! There is old china with rare devices, set out on the carved buffet; there are long and indolent lounges to throw yourself upon; there is an admirable sideboard, plentifully stored with good viands; there is a smell as of old wine in the pantry; and finally, in one corner, there is a dark little black-letter volume in golden clasps, entitled "Hawthorne: A Problem." It has delighted us; it has piqued a re-perusal; it has robbed us of a day, and made us a present of a whole year of thoughtfulness; it has bred great exhilaration and exultation with the remembrance that the architect of

---

From *The Letters of Herman Melville,* ed. by Merrell R. Davis and William H. Gilman (New Haven, 1960), pp. 123-125. A letter to Hawthorne dated 16(?) April(?) 1851.

Herman Melville

the Gables resides only six miles off, and not three thousand miles away, in England, say. We think the book, for pleasantness of running interest, surpasses the other works of the author. The curtains are more drawn; the sun comes in more; genialities peep out more. Were we to particularize what most struck us in the deeper passages, we would point out the scene where Clifford, for a moment, would fain throw himself forth from the window to join the procession; or the scene where the judge is left seated in his ancestral chair. Clifford is full of an awful truth throughout. He is conceived in the finest, truest spirit. He is no caricature. He is Clifford. And here we would say that, did circumstances permit, we should like nothing better than to devote an elaborate and careful paper to the full consideration and analysis of the purport and significance of what so strongly characterizes all of this author's writings. There is a certain tragic phase of humanity which, in our opinion, was never more powerfully embodied than by Hawthorne. We mean the tragicalness of human thought in its own unbiassed, native, and profounder workings. We think that into no recorded mind has the intense feeling of the visable truth ever entered more deeply than into this man's. By visable truth, we mean the apprehension of the absolute condition of present things as they strike the eye of the man who fears them not, though they do their worst to him,—the man who, like Russia or the British Empire, declares himself a sovereign nature (in himself) amid the powers of heaven, hell, and earth. He may perish; but so long as he exists he insists upon treating with all Powers upon an equal basis. If any of those other Powers choose to withhold certain secrets, let them; that does not impair my sovereignty in myself; that does not make me tributary. And perhaps, after all, there is *no* secret. We incline to think that the Problem of the Universe is like the Freemason's mighty secret, so terrible to all children. It turns out, at last, to consist in a triangle, a mallet, and an apron,—nothing more! We incline to think that God cannot explain His own secrets, and that He would like a little information upon certain points Himself. We mortals astonish Him as much as He us. But it is this *Being* of the matter; there lies the knot with which we choke ourselves. As soon as you say *Me,* a *God,* a *Nature,* so soon you jump off from your stool and hang from the beam. Yes, that word is the hangman. Take God out of the dictionary, and you would have Him in the street.

There is the grand truth about Nathaniel Hawthorne. He says NO! in thunder; but the Devil himself cannot make him say *yes.*

For all men who say *yes*, lie; and all men who say *no*,—why, they are in the happy condition of judicious, unincumbered travellers in Europe; they cross the frontiers into Eternity with nothing but a carpet-bag,—that is to say, the Ego. Whereas those *yes*-gentry, they travel with heaps of baggage, and, damn them! they will never get through the Custom House. What's the reason, Mr. Hawthorne, that in the last stages of metaphysics a fellow always falls to *swearing* so? I could rip an hour. You see, I began with a little criticism extracted for your benefit from the "Pittsfield Secret Review," and here I have landed in Africa.

Walk down one of these mornings and see me. No nonsense; come. Remember me to Mrs. Hawthorne and the children.

H. Melville.

P.S. The marriage of Phoebe with the daguerreotypist is a fine stroke, because of his turning out to be a *Maule*. If you pass Hepzibah's cent-shop, buy me a Jim Crow (fresh) and send it to me by Ned Higgins.

Anonymous

Exquisite Beauty of Finish

Ticknor, Reed, and Fields have issued *The House of the Seven Gables*, a Romance, by NATHANIEL HAWTHORNE, which is strongly marked with the bold and unique characteristics that have given its author such a brilliant position among American novelists. The scene, which is laid in the old Puritanic town of Salem, extends from the period of the witchcraft excitement to the present time, connecting the legends of the ancient superstition with the recent marvels of animal magnetism, and affording full scope for the indulgence of the most weird and sombre fancies. Destitute of the high-wrought manifestations of passion which distinguished the "Scarlet Letter," it is more terrific in its conception, and not less intense in its execution, but exquisitely relieved by charming portraitures of character, and quaint and comic descriptions of social eccentricities. A deep vein of reflection underlies the whole narrative, often rising naturally to the surface, and revealing the strength of the foundation on which the subtle, aerial inventions of the author are erected. His frequent dashes of humor gracefully blend with the monotone of the story, and soften the harsher colors

From *Harper's New Monthly Magazine,* vol. 2, May 1851, pp. 854-855.

in which he delights to clothe his portentous conceptions. In no former production of his pen, are his unrivalled powers of description displayed to better advantage. The rusty wooden house in Pyncheon-street, with its seven sharp-pointed gables, and its huge clustered chimney—the old elm tree before the door—the grassy yard seen through the lattice-fence, with its enormous fertility of burdocks—and the green moss on the slopes of the roof, with the flowers growing aloft in the air in the nook between two of the gables—present a picture to the eye as distinct as if our childhood had been passed in the shadow of the old weather-beaten edifice. Nor are the characters of the story drawn with less sharp and vigorous perspective. They stand out from the canvas as living realities. In spite of the supernatural drapery in which they are enveloped, they have such a genuine expression of flesh and blood, that we can not doubt we have known them all our days. They have the air of old acquaintance—only we wonder how the artist got them to sit for their likenesses. The grouping of these persons is managed with admirable artistic skill. Old Maid Pyncheon, concealing under her verjuice scowl the unutterable tenderness of a sister—her woman-hearted brother, on whose sensitive nature had fallen such a strange blight—sweet and beautiful Phebe, the noble village-maiden, whose presence is always like that of some shining angel—the dreamy, romantic descendant of the legendary wizard —the bold, bad man of the world, reproduced at intervals in the bloody Colonel, and the unscrupulous Judge—wise old Uncle Venner—and inappeasable Ned Higgins—are all made to occupy the place on the canvas which shows the lights and shades of their character in the most impressive contrast, and contributes to the wonderful vividness and harmony of the grand historical picture. On the whole, we regard "The House of the Seven Gables," though it exhibits no single scenes that may not be matched in depth and pathos by some of Mr. Hawthorne's previous creations, as unsurpassed by any thing he has yet written, in exquisite beauty of finish, in the skillful blending of the tragic and comic, and in the singular life-like reality with which the wildest traditions of the Puritanic age are combined with the every-day incidents of modern society.

[Rufus W. Griswold]

The Purest Piece of Imagination in our Prose Literature

Mr. Hawthorne's last work is *The House of Seven Gables,* a romance of the present day. It is not less original, not less striking, not less powerful, than The Scarlet Letter. We doubt indeed whether he has elsewhere surpassed either of the three strongly contrasted characters of the book. An innocent and joyous child-woman, Phœbe Pyncheon, comes from a farm-house into the grand and gloomy old mansion where her distant relation, Hepzibah Pyncheon, an aristocratical and fearfully ugly but kind-hearted unmarried woman of sixty, is just coming down from her faded state to keep in one of her drawing-rooms a small shop, that she may be able to maintain an elder brother who is every moment expected home from a prison to which in his youth he had been condemned unjustly, and in the silent solitude of which he has kept some lineaments of gentleness while his hair has grown white, and a sense of beauty while his brain has become disordered and his heart has been crushed and all present influences of beauty have been quite shut out. The House of Seven Gables is the purest piece of imagination in our prose literature.

From *The International Magazine,* vol. 3, May 1851, p. 159.

[Andrew Preston Peabody]

The Most Successful of His Romances

Of our author's "Romances," (for he affects that title, and we could suggest no better,) we suppose that "The House of the Seven Gables" has been, and we think that it deserves to be, the most successful with the public. The sentiment to which it gives expression is, (in his own words,) "that the wrong-doing of one generation lives into the successive ones, and, divesting itself of every temporary advantage, becomes a pure and uncontrollable mischief;" and he speaks, in the same sentence, "of the folly of tumbling down an avalanche of ill-gotten gold, or real estate, on the heads of an unfortunate posterity, thereby to maim and crush them, until the accumulated mass shall be scattered abroad in its original atoms."

. . .

The leading *dramatis personæ* have all been named, and the story may be told in brief. Hepzibah's brother is pardoned and sent back to her, dwarfed in intellect, enfeebled in body, depen-

From the *North American Review,* vol. 76, Jan. 1853, p. 233-237.

[Andrew Preston Peabody]

dent as a child of tender years, and the sole study of her life now is to soothe his petulance, to gratify his morbid tastes and appetites, and to woo back the intellect that has been prison-bound so long. Judge Pyncheon persists in seeking an interview with him, and dies, by the sudden visitation of God, in the very room and chair, and in the precise manner, in which the earlier heads of the family had been summoned to their account. The brother is cleared from the suspicion, which strong circumstantial evidence might well have cast upon him, of being his kinsman's murderer. It subsequently appears that the Judge had been the means, (as Hepzibah had never been unaware,) of arranging the evidence, which wrongfully consigned the brother to an almost lifelong incarceration, and had, through machinations of a like character, obtained possession of the great bulk of the family estate. The news of the death of the Judge's only son supervenes almost immediately upon his own death; and the occupants of the old house are the legal heirs of the childless intestate. Phœbe, a Pyncheon only in name, but inheriting from her mother a life unshadowed by the gloomy state and the respectable iniquity of her paternal ancestry, marries the daguerreotypist, who turns out to be the rightful representative of old Matthew Maule. The curse expires in their union; the prisoner, on whose deadened faculties the shadow of the Judge had lain as an incubus, draws a new lease of life from his kinsman's death; and he and his sister quit the old house for the judge's country-seat, under the kind tutelage of Phœbe and her bridegroom.

The successive scenes of this bold and startling fiction are portrayed with a vividness and power unsurpassed, and rarely equalled. The terrible Nemesis that waits on the extortion of the ancestor, and pursues the wages of his iniquity till the injured family receives its own again, reminds one of the inexorable fate of the Greek tragedy; and, in describing the successive footfalls of the angel of retribution in that ill-starred mansion, the author rises into a fearful sublimity worthy of the theme. In other portions, the narrative is sprightly, quaint, and droll, the dialogues seldom otherwise than natural and well managed, (though the daguerreotypist talks more than anybody but Phœbe could care to hear,) and the *denouement* free, for the most part, from abruptness and improbability. To many readers, the book has an additional charm, from its truth in numberless minutiæ to life, speech, manners, and appearances, as they were in and about Salem thirty years ago. We should have recognized the locality under any disguise whatever of names or pretexts. Hepzibah, the ancient house, the peculiar fitting up of the shop, the customers young and old, Uncle Venner the wood-sawyer, nay, the outer man, (not the oleaginousness of conscience, we trust,) of Judge Pyncheon, and a hundred nameless objects and incidents, recall to our memory Salem, as we knew it, when, before the welding of place to place by railroads, there were local peculiarities.

Henry Theodore Tuckerman

A Flemish Painting

"The House of the Seven Gables" is a more elaborate and harmonious realization of these characteristics. The scenery, tone, and personages of the story are imbued with a local authenticity which is not, for an instant, impaired by the imaginative charm of romance. We seem to breathe, as we read, the air, and be surrounded by the familiar objects, of a New England town. The interior of the House, each article described within it,—from the quaint table to the miniature by Malbone,—every product of the old garden, the street-scenes that beguile the eyes of poor Clifford, as he looks out of the arched window, the noble elm and the gingerbread figures at the little shop-window,—all have the significance that belongs to reality when seized upon by art. In these details we have the truth, simplicity, and exact imitation of the Flemish painters. So life-like in the minutiæ and so picturesque in general effect are these sketches of still-life, that they are daguerreotyped in the reader's mind, and form a distinct and changeless background, the light and shade of which give admirable effect to the action of the story; occasional touches of humor,

---

From *The Southern Literary Messenger,* vol. 17, June 1851, pp. 348-349.

introduced with exquisite tact, relieve the grave undertone of the narrative, and form vivacious and quaint images which might readily be transferred to canvas—so effectively are they drawn in words; take, for instance, the street-musician and the Pyncheon fowls, the Judge balked of his kiss over the counter, Phœbe reading to Clifford in the garden, or the old maid in her lonely chamber, gazing on the sweet lineaments of her unfortunate brother.

Nor is Hawthorne less successful in those pictures that are drawn exclusively for the mind's eye, and are obvious to sensation rather than the actual vision. Were a New England Sunday, breakfast, old mansion, easterly storm, or the morning after it clears, ever so well described? The skill in atmosphere we have noted in his lighter sketches is also as apparent: around and within the principal scene of this romance, there hovers an alternating melancholy and brightness which is born of genuine moral life; no contrasts can be imagined of this kind, more eloquent to a sympathetic mind than that between the inward consciousness and external appearance of Hepzibah, or Phœbe and Clifford, or the Judge. They respectively symbolize the poles of human existence, and are fine studies for the psychologist. Yet this attraction is subservient to fidelity to local characteristics. Clifford represents, though in its most tragic imaginable phase, the man of fine organization and true sentiment environed by the material realities of New England life; his plausible uncle is the type of New England selfishness, glorified by respectable conformity and wealth; Phœbe is the ideal of genuine, efficient, yet loving female character in the same latitude; Uncle Venner we regard as one of the most fresh yet familiar portraits in the book; all denizens of our eastern provincial towns must have known such a philosopher; and Holgrave embodies Yankee acuteness and hardihood redeemed by integrity and enthusiasm. The contact of these most judiciously selected and highly characteristic elements brings out, not only many beautiful revelations of nature, but elucidates interesting truth; magnetism and socialism are admirably introduced; family tyranny in its most revolting form is powerfully exemplified; the distinction between a mental and a heartfelt interest in another, clearly unfolded; and the tenacious and hereditary nature of moral evil, impressively shadowed forth. The natural refinements of the human heart, the holiness of a ministry of disinterested affection, the gracefulness of the homeliest services when irradiated by cheerfulness and benevolence, are illustrated with singular beauty. "He," says our author, speaking of Clifford, "had no right to be a martyr; and, beholding him so fit to be happy, and so feeble for all other purposes, a generous, strong, and noble spirit would, methinks, have been ready to sacrifice what little enjoyment it might have planned for itself,—*it would have flung down the hopes so paltry in its regard—if thereby the wintry blasts of our rude sphere might come tempered to such a man:*" and elsewhere: "Phœbe's presence made a home about her,—that very sphere which the outcast, the prisoner, the potentate, the wretch beneath mankind, the wretch aside from it, or the wretch above it, instinctively pines after,—a home. She was real! Holding her hand, you felt something; a tender something; a substance and a warm one; *and so long as you could feel its grasp, soft as it was, you might be certain that your place was good in the whole sympathetic chain of human nature.* The world was no longer a delusion."

Thus narrowly, yet with reverence, does Hawthorne analyze the delicate traits of human sentiment and character; and opens vistas into that beautiful and unexplored world of love and thought that exists in every human being, though overshadowed by material circumstance and technical duty. This, as we have before said, is his great service; digressing every now and then, from the main drift of his story, he takes evident delight in expatiating on phases of character and general traits of life, or in bringing into strong relief the more latent facts of consciousness. Perhaps the union of the philosophic tendency with the poetic instinct is the great charm of his genius. It is common for American critics to estimate the interest of all writings by their comparative glow, vivacity, and rapidity of action: somewhat of the restless temperament and enterprising life of the nation infects its taste: such terms as "quiet," "gentle," and "tasteful," are equivocal, when applied in this country to a book; and yet they may envelop the rarest energy of thought and depth of insight as well as earnestness of feeling: these qualities, in reflective minds, are too real to find melodramatic development; they move as calmly as summer waves, or glow as noiselessly as the firmament; but not the less grand and mighty is their essence; to realize it, the spirit of contemplation, and the recipient mood of sympathy must be evoked; for it is not external but moral excitement that is proposed; and we deem one of Hawthorne's most felicitous merits, that of so patiently educing artistic beauty and moral interest from life and nature, without the least sacrifice of intellectual dignity.

The healthy spring of life is typified in Phœbe so freshly as to magnetize the feelings as well as engage the perceptions of the reader; its intellectual phase finds expression in Holgrave, while the state of Clifford, when relieved of the nightmare that oppressed his sensitive temperament, the author justly compares to an Indian summer of the soul. Across the path of these beings of genuine flesh and blood, who constantly appeal to our most humane sympathies, or rather around their consciousness and history, flits the pale, mystic figure of Alice, whose invisible music and legendary fate overflow with a graceful and attractive superstition, yielding an Ariel-like melody to the more solemn and cheery strains of the whole composition. Among the apt though incidental touches of the picture, the idea of making the music-grinder's monkey an epitome of avarice, the daguerreotype a test of latent character, and the love of the reformer Holgrave for the genially practical Phœbe win him to conservatism, strike us as remarkably natural, yet quite as ingenious and charming as philosophical. We may add that the same pure, even, unexaggerated and perspicuous style of diction that we have recognized in his previous writing is maintained in this.

As earth and sky appear to blend at the horizon, though we cannot define the point of contact, things seen and unseen, the actual and the spiritual, mind and matter, what is within and what is without our consciousness, have a line of union, and, like the color of the iris, are lost in each other. About this equator of life the genius of Hawthorne delights to hover as its appropriate sphere; whether indulging a vein of Spenserian allegory, Hogarth sketching, Goldsmith domesticity, or Godwin metaphysics, it is around the boundary of the possible that he most freely expatiates; the realities and the mysteries of life to his vision are scarcely ever apart; they act and react so as to yield dramatic hints or vistas of sentiment. Time broods with touching solemnity over his imagination; the function of conscience awes while it occupies his mind; the delicate and the profound in love, and the awful beauty of death transfuse his meditation; and these supernal he loves to link with terrestrial influences, to hallow a graphic description by a sacred association, or to brighten a commonplace occasion with the scintillations of humor—thus vivifying or chastening the "light of common day."

Anonymous

Truthful Delineations of Character

The House of the Seven Gables. A romance. By NATHANIEL HAWTHORNE. Boston: Ticknor, Reed & Fields. 1851. Mr. Hawthorne is rapidly making himself a high reputation, as a writer of prose fiction. He is a tale writer, rather than a novelist, and exhibits some very peculiar endowments in this character. He has a rare and delicate fancy, with an imagination capable, in particular, of that curious distribution of light and shade—"that little glooming light, most like a shade,"—which constitutes the singular faculty of some of the most remarkable of the Italian painters. He is truthful, also, in his delineations of character, though his range is a limited one. He enters, with the art of Sterne, into the heart of his single captive, and, with exquisite adroitness, unfolds to you, and to the victim's self, the hurts of the secret nerve, its morbid condition, and how it operates upon, and affects by sympathy, the whole system. In these revelations, our author shows himself a minute philosopher. He goes farther than the simple delineation of the sore and secret places—he shows you why they became sore, and how they failed to keep their secrets from him. As a writer of

From *The Southern Quarterly Review,* vol. 20, July 1851, pp. 265-266.

prose fancies, fresh and delicate, of simple truths of the heart, which are obscure, in other hands, only from the absence of those exquisite antennæ which he employs, he exhibits a grace and felicity which show him to be a master. His province is peculiarly this fine one of the heart, with its subtler conditions, its eccentric moods, the result of secret weaknesses or secret consciousnesses, which it dare not confess and dare not overcome—its aberrations of soul or temper—its morbid passions, which fester without action, and are thus quite as vicious as if they had become developed by the actual commission of crime. Of the particular story before us, we have only to add that it exhibits happily the characteristic faculty of the author, in the delineation of morbid and peculiar conditions—in the curious distribution of light and shadow, and in the utterance of graceful and happy fancies, in close connection with moral philosophies and mental feelings, which are at once true to nature and agreeable to art. As a story, the "House of the Seven Gables" will probably prove less attractive to the general reader than the "Scarlet Letter," as exhibiting a less concentrative power; but it is a more truthful book, and, if less ambitious in plan and manner, is not less earnest of purpose, nor less efficient in the varieties of character.

E. D. Forgues
(Translation by Roger Asselineau)

A French View

The House of the Seven Gables is, in our opinion, if not [Hawthorne's] best work, at least the one in which he has made most use of what constitutes his particular originality: the gift of acting powerfully, by the force of his own imagination, on the imagination of his readers. The story he tells is built on a rather well-worn theme: the chronicle of two hostile families. There is the question of a lost document whose possession involves the acquirement of an immense fortune. There is the hereditary fatality which, for four or five generations, continuously opposes the members of two clans; there is an old house peopled with tragic memories; an old portrait set in an old panelling and which a bizarre will has fixed there forever. This portrait is involved in the plot where it plays the role that ghosts played before the invention of oil painting. It is the portrait which hides the lost document, and it is the portrait which holds in suspense and then unravels the chain of events. In fact, we have here all the hackneyed ingredients of ghost stories, the kind of story that Walter Scott, Lewis, Mrs. Radcliffe and Washington Irving, not to speak

From *Revue des Deux Mondes,* vol. 14 (April 15, 1852), pp. 356-357.

of Maturin, Hoffmann and many others besides, have often written. Nonetheless, if the content of the story is dated, Hawthorne has shown unquestionable talent in the choice of dim colors, of mysterious harmonies, of half glimpsed shapes, of strange insights which have enabled him to give new vigor to this overworked theme, and to introduce new elements into it, to unite to the prosaic details of contemporary life poetic echoes from the past.

At the beginning of the book, the intelligent reader is soon made aware that he must not look for more than can be found; he must not look for originality of plot, but for great charm of detail and an acute sensitivity to the relationship existing between the outside world and the inner world in each one of us. From that moment on, he will fall completely under the forceful influence of a carefully and intelligently finished work of art. He will admire, in the gradually increasing intensity of the effects, at first treated with great economy, a sustained progression. He will feel the extent to which the contrast of the rather ironical forms of the modern novelist adds to the fantastic effects with which the author gradually means to surround you. He will recognize the superiority of the writer above all in the originality of cleverly imagined characters whose particular type and sharply drawn individuality here appear in the world of fiction for the first time. He will see this in the figure of Hepzibah Pyncheon, the old spinster of aristocratic origins, who has been forced by poverty to open a haberdashery shop, and whose moral sufferings in the midst of this decline awaken, as much as the most poignant tragedy, a melancholy sense of sympathy in the reader. He will recognize it equally in the analysis of a strange form of madness, that of the brother of Hepzibah, born with all the instincts of a highly refined sensualism, and whose youth, as a result of infernal scheming, was wasted away in a prison (where in fact he lost his reason). He will recognize it above all in that delicacy of execution and perfection of finish which Hawthorne combines with a rare breadth of composition, and an astonishing liberty in the disposition of groups, light and color. His philosophical and poetic instincts, for he is undoubtedly both a philosopher and a poet, are always sufficiently predominant to keep him on a certain high level, and forearm him against the futile prolixity and trivial details of the modern novel.

2. A Grudging Admirer: Henry James

Henry James

A Magnificent Fragment

The House of the Seven Gables was written at Lenox, among the mountains of Massachusetts, a village nestling, rather loosely, in one of the loveliest corners of New England, to which Hawthorne had betaken himself after the success of *The Scarlet Letter* became conspicuous, in the summer of 1850, and where he occupied for two years an uncomfortable little red house which is now pointed out to the inquiring stranger. The inquiring stranger is now a frequent figure at Lenox, for the place has suffered the process of lionisation. It has become a prosperous watering-place, or at least (as there are no waters), as they say in America, a summer-resort. It is a brilliant and generous landscape, and thirty years ago a man of fancy, desiring to apply himself, might have found both inspiration and tranquillity there. Hawthorne found so much of both that he wrote more during his two years of residence at Lenox than at any period of his career. He began with *The House of the Seven Gables*, which was finished in the early part of 1851. This is the longest of his three American novels, it is the most elaborate, and in the judgment of some persons it is the

---

From *Hawthorne,* English Men of Letters Series, London, 1879.

finest. It is a rich, delightful, imaginative work, larger and more various than its companions, and full of all sorts of deep intentions, of interwoven threads of suggestion. But it is not so rounded and complete as *The Scarlet Letter*; it has always seemed to me more like a prologue to a great novel than a great novel itself. I think this is partly owing to the fact that the subject, the *donnée*, as the French say, of the story, does not quite fill it out, and that we get at the same time an impression of certain complicated purposes on the author's part, which seem to reach beyond it. I call it larger and more various than its companions, and it has indeed a greater richness of tone and density of detail. The colour, so to speak, of *The House of the Seven Gables* is admirable. But the story has a sort of expansive quality which never wholly fructifies, and as I lately laid it down, after reading it for the third time, I had a sense of having interested myself in a magnificent fragment. Yet the book has a great fascination, and of all of those of its author's productions which I have read over while writing this sketch, it is perhaps the one that has gained most by reperusal. If it be true of the others that the pure, natural quality of the imaginative strain is their great merit, this is at least as true of *The House of the Seven Gables*, the charm of which is in a peculiar degree of the kind that we fail to reduce to its grounds—like that of the sweetness of a piece of music, or the softness of fine September weather. It is vague, indefinable, ineffable; but it is the sort of thing we must always point to in justification of the high claim that we make for Hawthorne. In this case of course its vagueness is a drawback, for it is difficult to point to ethereal beauties; and if the reader whom we have wished to inoculate with our admiration informs us after looking a while that he perceives nothing in particular, we can only reply that, in effect, the object is a delicate one.

The House of the Seven Gables comes nearer being a picture of contemporary American life than either of its companions; but on this ground it would be a mistake to make a large claim for it. It cannot be too often repeated that Hawthorne was not a realist. He had a high sense of reality—his Note-Books superabundantly testify to it; and fond as he was of jotting down the items that make it up, he never attempted to render exactly or closely the actual facts of the society that surrounded him. I have said—I began by saying—that his pages were full of its spirit, and of a certain reflected light that springs from it; but I was careful to add that the reader must look for his local and national quality between the lines of his writing and in the *indirect* testimony of his tone, his accent, his temper, of his very omissions and suppressions. *The House of the Seven Gables* has, however, more literal actuality than the others, and if it were not too fanciful an account of it, I should say that it renders, to an initiated reader, the impression of a summer afternoon in an elm-shadowed New England town. It leaves upon the mind a vague correspondence to some such reminiscence, and in stirring up the association it renders it delightful. The comparison is to the honour of the New England town, which gains in it more than it bestows. The shadows of the elms, in *The House of the Seven Gables,* are exceptionally dense and cool; the summer afternoon is peculiarly still and beautiful; the atmosphere has a delicious warmth, and the long daylight seems to pause and rest. But the mild provincial quality is there, the mixture of shabbiness and freshness, the paucity of ingredients. The end of an old race—this is the situation that Hawthorne has depicted, and he has been admirably inspired in the choice of the figures in whom he seeks to interest us. They are all figures rather than characters—they are all pictures rather than persons. But if their reality is light and vague, it is sufficient, and it is in harmony with the low relief and dimness of outline of the objects that surround them. They are all types, to the author's mind, of something general, of something that is bound up with the history, at large, of families and individuals, and each of them is the centre of a cluster of those ingenious and meditative musings, rather melancholy, as a general thing, than joyous, which melt into the current and texture of the story and give it a kind of moral richness. A grotesque old spinster, simple, childish, penniless, very humble at heart, but rigidly conscious of her pedigree; an amiable bachelor, of an epicurean temperament and an enfeebled intellect, who has passed twenty years of his life in penal confinement for a crime of which he was unjustly pronounced guilty; a sweet-natured and bright-faced young girl from the country, a poor relation of these two ancient decrepitudes, with whose moral mustiness her modern freshness and soundness are contrasted; a young man still more modern, holding the latest opinions, who has sought his fortune up and down the world, and, though he has not found it, takes a genial and enthusiastic view of the future: these, with two or three remarkable accessory figures, are the persons concerned in the little drama. The drama is a small one, but as Hawthorne does not put it before us for its own superficial sake for the dry facts of the case, but for something in it which he holds to be symbolic and of large application, something that points a moral and that it behoves us to remember, the scenes in the rusty wooden house whose gables give its name to the story, have something of the dignity both of history and of tragedy. Miss Hephzibah [sic] Pyncheon, dragging out a disappointed life in her paternal dwelling, finds herself obliged in her old age to open a little shop for the sale of penny toys and gingerbread. This is the central incident of the tale, and, as Hawthorne relates it, it is an incident of the most impressive magnitude and most touching interest. Her dishonoured and vague-minded brother is released from prison at the same moment, and returns to the ancestral roof to deepen her perplexities. But, on the other hand, to alleviate them, and to introduce a breath of the air of the outer world into this long unventilated interior, the little country cousin also arrives, and proves the good angel of the feebly distracted household. All this episode is exquisite—admirably conceived, and executed with a kind of humorous tenderness, an equal sense of everything in it that is picturesque, touching, ridiculous, worthy of the highest praise. Hephzibah Pyncheon, with her near-sighted scowl, her rusty joints, her antique turban, her map of a great territory to the eastward which ought to have belonged to her family, her vain terrors and scruples and resentments, the inaptitude and repugnance of an ancient gentlewoman to the vulgar little commerce which a cruel fate has compelled her to engage in—Hephzibah Pyncheon is a masterly picture. I repeat that she is a picture, as her companions are pictures; she is a charming piece of descriptive writing, rather than a dramatic exhibition. But she is described, like her companions too, so subtly and lovingly that we enter into her virginal old heart and stand with her behind her abominable little counter. Clifford Pyncheon is a still more remarkable conception, though he is perhaps not so vividly depicted. It was a figure needing a much more subtle touch, however, and it was of the essence of his character to be vague and unemphasised. Nothing can be more charming than the manner in which the soft, bright, active presence of Phœbe Pyncheon is indicated, or than the account of her relations with the poor dimly sentient kinsman for whom her light-handed sisterly offices, in the evening of a melancholy life, are a revelation of lost possibilities of happiness. 'In her aspect', Hawthorne says of the young girl, 'there was a familiar gladness, and a holiness that you could play with, and yet reverence it as much as ever. She was like a prayer offered up in the homeliest beauty of one's mother-tongue. Fresh was Phœbe, moreover, and airy, and sweet in her apparel; as if nothing that she wore—neither her gown, nor her small straw bonnet, nor her little kerchief, any more than her snowy stockings—had ever been put on before; or if worn, were all the fresher for it, and with a fragrance as if they had lain among the rose-buds.' Of the influence of her maidenly salubrity upon poor Clifford, Hawthorne gives the prettiest description, and then, breaking off suddenly, renounces the attempt in language which, while pleading its inadequacy, conveys an exquisite satisfaction to the reader. I quote the passage for the sake of its extreme felicity, and of the charming image with which it concludes.

> But we strive in vain to put the idea into words. No adequate expression of the beauty and profound pathos with which it impresses us is attainable. This being, made only for happiness, and heretofore so miserably failing to be happy—his tendencies so hideously thwarted that some unknown time ago, the delicate springs of his character, never morally or intellectually strong, had given way, and he was now imbecile—this poor forlorn voyager from the Islands of the Blest, in a frail bark, on a tempestuous sea, had been flung by the last mountain-wave of his shipwreck, into a quiet harbour. There, as he lay more than half lifeless on the strand, the fragrance of an earthly rosebud had come to his nostrils, and, as odours will, had summoned up reminiscences or visions of all the living and breathing beauty amid which he should have had his home. With his native susceptibility of happy influences, he inhales the slight ethereal rapture into his soul, and expires!

I have not mentioned the personage in *The House of the Seven Gables* upon whom Hawthorne evidently bestowed most pains, and whose portrait is the most elaborate in the book; partly because he is, in spite of the space he occupies, an accessory figure, and partly because, even more than the others, he is what I have called a picture rather than a character. Judge Pyncheon is an ironical portrait, very richly and broadly executed, very sagaciously composed and rendered—the portrait of a superb, full-blown hypocrite, a large-based, full-nurtured Pharisee, bland, urbane, impressive, diffusing about him a 'sultry' warmth of benevolence, as the author calls it again and again, and basking in the noontide of prosperity and the consideration of society; but in reality hard, gross, and ignoble. Judge Pyncheon is an elaborate piece of description, made up of a hundred admirable touches, in which satire is always winged with fancy, and fancy is linked with a deep sense of reality. It is difficult to say whether Hawthorne followed a model in describing Judge Pyncheon; but it is tolerably obvious that the picture is an impression—a copious impression—of an individual. It has evidently a definite starting-point in fact, and the author is able to draw, freely and confidently, after the image established in his mind. Holgrave, the modern young man, who has been a Jack-of-all-trades and is at the period of the story a daguerreotypist, is an attempt to render a kind of national type—that of the young citizen of the United States whose fortune is simply in his lively intelligence, and who stands naked, as it were, unbiased and unencumbered alike, in the centre of the far-stretching level of American life. Holgrave is intended as a contrast; his lack of traditions, his democratic stamp, his condensed experience, are opposed to the desiccated prejudices and exhausted vitality of the race of which poor feebly-scowling, rusty-jointed Hephzibah is the most heroic representative. It is perhaps a pity that Hawthorne should not have proposed to himself to give the old Pyncheon-qualities some embodiment which would help them to balance more fairly with the elastic properties of the young daguerreotypist—should not have painted a lusty conservative to match his strenuous radical. As it is, the mustiness and mouldiness of the tenants of the House of the Seven Gables crumble away rather too easily. Evidently, however, what Hawthorne designed to represent was not the struggle between an old society and a new, for in this case he would have given the old one a better chance; but simply, as I have said, the shrinkage and extinction of a family. This appealed to his imagination; and the idea of long perpetuation and survival always appears to have filled him with a kind of horror and disapproval. Conservative, in a certain degree, as he was himself, and fond of retrospect and quietude and the mellowing influences of time, it is singular how often one encounters in his writings some expression of mistrust of old houses, old institutions, long lines of descent. He was disposed apparently to allow a very moderate measure in these respects, and he condemns the dwelling of the Pyncheons to disappear from the face of the earth because it has been standing a couple of hundred years. In this he was an American of Americans; or rather he was more American than many of his countrymen, who, though they are accustomed to work for the short run rather than the long, have often a lurking esteem for things that show the marks of having lasted. I will add that Holgrave is one of the few figures, among those which Hawthorne created, with regard to which the absence of the realistic mode of treatment is felt as a loss. Holgrave is not sharply enough characterised; he lacks features; he is not an individual, but a type. But my last word about this admirable novel must not be a restrictive one. It is a large and generous production, pervaded with that vague hum, that indefinable echo, of the whole multitudinous life of man, which is the real sign of a great work of fiction.

3. XXth Century Interpretations

Frederick C. Crews

A Psychoanalytical Interpretation

The problem is, to be sure, relatively inconspicuous in *The House of the Seven Gables*, which can engage the reader successfully either in its love story, its picturesque Salem history, its Yankee humor, its romantic legend, its modern realism, its melodrama, or even its few moments of Gothic terror. Only when he tries to find aesthetic order in these motley effects does the critic begin to see that there is something fundamentally contradictory in Hawthorne's romance. Why does the announced moral purpose of showing that "the wrong-doing of one generation lives into the successive ones, and . . . becomes a pure and uncontrollable mischief" (III, 14) get dissolved in the "dear home-loveliness and satisfaction" that Sophia Hawthorne discerned in the final pages? Is it because Hawthorne's true intention was comic and sentimental all along? But if so, how do we account for the primitive intensity with which both Hawthorne and his "good" characters seem to despise and fear the villain of the story, Judge Jaffrey

---

From *The Sins of the Fathers: Hawthorne's Psychological Themes*, pp. 172-193. Copyright © 1966 by Frederick C. Crews. Reprinted by permission of Oxford University Press, Inc.

Pyncheon? Why is Holgrave, the daguerreotypist, author, and social radical, represented as being both self-sufficient and in desperate need of marriage to the busy little conformist, Phoebe Pyncheon? Why does the mere death of Jaffrey Pyncheon, rather than any conscious moral penance, free the modern Pyncheons from the real or metaphorical curse that has dogged their family for two centuries? Why does Hawthorne feel obliged to dwell whimsically, but at disconcerting length, on a number of largely trivial symbols —a house, an elm, a well, a spring, a mirror, some posies, a garden, some hens, some bees? Why must he apologize over and over for being tedious or inconsistent in tone? Why does he use his plot for an extensive yet partly covert review of all the scandals and weaknesses in his own family history? And why, in his avowed attempt at writing a popular romance, does he give such prominence to two characters, Hepzibah and Clifford Pyncheon, for whom nearly all the possibilities of life are already exhausted?

In order to take a sufficiently inclusive view of *The House of the Seven Gables* we must both examine and look beyond Hawthorne's surface emphasis. The book is not a diabolical exercise in deceit; Hawthorne means, or would like to mean, what he says about his characters and their doings. But his deeper hints of characterization, his imagery, and the direction of his plot all bespeak an overriding concern with an unstated theme. The ending, which strikes the modern reader as morally complacent, is in fact psychologically urgent, an ingeniously ambiguous gesture of expiation for a dominant idea that has been warping the book's direction. When the obsessed Holgrave, the character who most nearly resembles Hawthorne-as-artist, swears to Phoebe that he has already turned conservative for her sake, he is making a declaration on behalf of the entire romance. *The House of the Seven Gables* "turns conservative" as a way of evading its deepest implications —the same fantasy-implications we have noted elsewhere.

Looking forward to Hawthorne's creative breakdown as well as backward to the tales mentioned in Chapter 9, we shall argue that on its autobiographical level *The House of the Seven Gables* is "about" the risks of artistic imagination, which are simply the risks of seizure by unconscious wishes. Roughly the same debate between fantasy and inhibition recurs in each of the late romances, and always with the same outcome. Since forbidden thoughts inevitably smirk through the best efforts at conventionality, the whole enterprise of fiction must be symbolically renounced—or, in the case of the four abortive romances, quite literally renounced. We shall be able to show that those last plots are not broken off because Hawthorne became sick or weary or morally confused, but because they too frankly embody the theme which is barely kept under control in the book at hand.

In one respect it is generally agreed that this romance has an autobiographical significance. The Pyncheon forebears, whose history opens the plot and is resumed at several points, are unmistakable representatives of the Hathornes; hence the mixture of nostalgia and resentment in their portrayal. Hawthorne's customary charges against his ancestors—of religious hypocrisy, social tyranny, and moral abuse—are leveled against the Pyncheons, and specific family shames such as the Salem witch hangings are exploited for the announced theme of inherited guilt. The decline of the Pyncheons is half-seriously attributed to a curse which is closely modeled on one that the accused witch Sarah Good supposedly laid upon John Hathorne (really upon Nicholas Noyes). And the disinherited modern Pyncheons resemble Hawthorne in regretting the gradual loss of the authority under which their family's historic crimes were perpetrated. In this light it is significant that the plot works toward a symbolic expiation and a reversal of bad fortune for the sympathetic Pyncheons. Hawthorne can laugh at the worthless "eastern claims" of the Pyncheon-Hathornes, but his satire is blunted by the fact that Hepzibah and Clifford come into easy circumstances, while the "guilty" remnant of Puritan days, the arch-villain Jaffrey Pyncheon, is conveniently and mysteriously put to death. The providential ending, in other words, amounts to a wishful settling of old scores on Hawthorne's part.[1]

The very fact that Jaffrey Pyncheon *is* a villain—one who is treated even less generously than Roger Chillingworth—deserves pondering in view of the meaning of ancestral tyrants throughout Hawthorne's fiction. Jaffrey is a slightly attenuated reincarnation of the original Colonel Pyncheon, the family's father; and the entire romance prior to his death is oppressed with a sense of fierce authority and inhibition. Jaffrey's effect on his cousins is exactly that of Colonel Pyncheon's portrait, which, with its "stern, immitigable features," acts as "the Evil Genius of his family," ensuring that "no good thoughts or purposes could ever spring up and blossom" (III, 36) under his gaze. By now we might feel entitled to surmise from such phrases that Jaffrey's role in *The House of the Seven Gables* is paternal, and that the two sets of characters

---

[1] It is also noteworthy that Clifford Pyncheon has been imprisoned for a crime resembling the White murder case—a page of recent history that Hawthorne found particularly shameful—but is later vindicated by the discovery that no murder took place at all.

who survive him are symbolically his children. There is in fact more than sufficient evidence for this reading. At present, however, let us rest content with the observation that Jaffrey's death is the central event of the plot, enabling one couple to have a euphoric escape and another couple to marry and become rich. Nor should we omit the effect of Jaffrey's death on Hawthorne himself. Whether or not Jaffrey is recognized as a father figure, the reader must surely acknowledge the clogged passion, the vindictive pleasure, expressed in that extraordinary chapter (18) which is given over to a fearful taunting of Jaffrey's corpse.

A mixture of awe and hatred is discernible through the entire rendering of Judge Pyncheon. His villainy is separated from his conscience by layers of self-esteem and public honor which seem to impress Hawthorne despite his moral disapproval of them. For Hawthorne as for Clifford and Hepzibah, Jaffrey is an imminent presence, an unspecified threat, rather than an active criminal. While he is alive his specific guilt can only be suggested in an elaborate, highly tentative metaphor. In some forgotten nook of the "stately edifice" of an important man's character, says Hawthorne,

> may lie a corpse, half decayed, and still decaying, and diffusing its death-scent all through the palace! The inhabitant will not be conscious of it, for it has long been his daily breath! Neither will the visitors, for they smell only the rich odors which the master sedulously scatters through the palace . . . Now and then, perchance, comes in a seer, before whose sadly gifted eye the whole structure melts into thin air, leaving only the hidden nook, the bolted closet, . . . or the deadly hole under the pavement, and the decaying corpse within. Here, then, we are to seek the true emblem of the man's character, and of the deed which gives whatever reality it possesses to his life. And, beneath the show of a marble palace, that pool of stagnant water, foul with many impurities, and, perhaps, tinged with blood,—that secret abomination, above which, possibly, he may say his prayers, without remembering it, —is this man's miserable soul! (III, 274)

Hawthorne makes it sufficiently clear that Jaffrey's case is being described here, yet the deviousness and Gothic gruesomeness of the accusation show a reluctance to approach the matter very closely. The metaphor, in declaring that only the sadly gifted eye of the seer can perceive Jaffrey's real nature, encourages us to look for repressed guilt or be left with specious appearances; yet Hawthorne himself is less willing than formerly to explain the nature and operation of that guilt. Even in death Jaffrey remains inscrutable and terrifying, resistant to the autopsy of motives that Hawthorne does not yet feel ready to undertake.

We do, of course, finally learn the exact circumstances that make Hawthorne "almost venture to say . . . that a daily guilt might have been acted by [Jaffrey], continually renewed . . . without his necessarily and at every moment being aware of it" (III, 273). Jaffrey has robbed his uncle, named Clifford; his uncle, witnessing the deed, has consequently died of shock; and Jaffrey has framed his cousin, young Clifford Pyncheon, for this supposed murder. Thus the ex-convict Clifford is, in the sense of Hawthorne's metaphor, Jaffrey's "corpse"—or, to use another word that is much emphasized, his "ghost." In this light the manner of Jaffrey's own death becomes ironically appropriate. As Alfred H. Marks persuasively argues, Hawthorne implies that Jaffrey's mysterious death is caused by the unexpected sight of the "ghost" Clifford Pyncheon.[2] It is likely that Jaffrey dies in the same way as his uncle. A Clifford, in this event, has caused the death of Jaffrey after Jaffrey has caused the death of a Clifford—a symmetry of justice reminiscent of "Roger Malvin's Burial."

To mention "Roger Malvin's Burial," however, is to measure the distance Hawthorne has traveled from the early 1830's. Jaffrey's guilt, unlike Reuben Bourne's, is never rendered in terms of observable behavior; at the moment of his death he is as imposing and impenetrable as ever. It would seem that Hawthorne is more anxious to avoid him than to understand him. Surely it is meaningful that Jaffrey dies offstage through no one's intention, and is only gingerly approached in death by the morbidly scornful narrator. We are nearing the strange world of the unfinished romances, where figures of authority receive sudden outbursts of unexplained authorial hatred and are savagely killed, not by their antagonists, but by "innocent" mischances of plotting. Filial obsession, in other words, is beginning to destroy objective characterization and moral interest.[3]

---

[2] See "Who Killed Judge Pyncheon? The Role of the Imagination in *The House of the Seven Gables*," *PMLA*, LXXI (June 1956), 355-69.
[3] The privacy of Hawthorne's filial concern may be gauged from another piece of veiled family biography. Jaffrey's death is immediately, we might almost say casually, followed by the death by cholera, in a foreign port, of his last direct heir. Hawthorne's own father died of a fever (first reported to be cholera) in Surinam—a fact that could hardly have been generally known to readers of *The House of the Seven Gables*. Thus Hawthorne stamps a paternal significance on Judge Pyncheon not for any instructive purpose, but because that is what secret fantasy demands.

Yet in a cryptic way *The House of the Seven Gables* deals extensively with moral and psychological affairs. Its "necromancies," we are told, may one day find their true meaning within "modern psychology" (III, 42). In various ways Hawthorne allows us to see the entire historical, social, and symbolic framework of the romance as pertaining to the question of individual guilt. The focal symbol of the House is endowed from the opening page with "a human countenance" (III, 17), and the struggle for possession of it follows familiar Hawthornian lines. The falsely accused wizard Matthew Maule has not been simply executed by his enemy, Colonel Pyncheon; he has been incorporated into the subsequent life of the House. The new structure "would include the home of the dead and buried wizard, and would thus afford the ghost of the latter a kind of privilege to haunt its new apartments . . ." (III, 21). Like the more strictly figurative "ruined wall" of *The Scarlet Letter*, the Pyncheon estate embodies a mental condition in which an uneasy re-enactment of guilt will be made necessary by the effort to avoid responsibility for that guilt. For all its political and social ramifications, the Maule-Pyncheon antagonism is chiefly a metaphor of imperfect repression.[4]

This imperfect repression is the agent of all the ironic justice in *The House of the Seven Gables*. Every tyrant is psychologically at the mercy of his victim; or, as Hawthorne puts it in his notebook, "All slavery is reciprocal" (*American Notebooks*, p. 107). The rule is first applied to the original Colonel Pyncheon, who dies while inaugurating the House he has built on the executed Matthew Maule's property. It is clear that the Colonel's "curse" of susceptibility to sudden death is nothing other than his guilt toward Maule. The pattern is repeated by Gervayse Pyncheon in the story told by Holgrave; this Pyncheon's greed makes him tacitly cooperate when the second Matthew Maule, supposedly in exchange for a valuable document, takes mesmeric control over his daughter and subsequently causes her death. And if Mark's theory is correct, Jaffrey Pyncheon is similarly enslaved to the oppressed Clifford, who is able to cause Jaffrey's death merely by entering his

---

[4] Note, for example, that the hereditary mesmeric power of the Maules, who are said to dominate the Pyncheons in "the topsy-turvy commonwealth of sleep" (III, 42), directly depends on the Pyncheons' continuing bad conscience. Holgrave, the last of the Maules, tells us this (III, 64), and Hawthorne speculates "whether each inheritor of the property—conscious of wrong, and failing to rectify it—did not commit anew the great guilt of his ancestor, and incur all its original responsibilities" (III, 34).

field of vision. In all these cases it is bad conscience, rather than arbitrary plotting on Hawthorne's part, that has exacted punishment for abuses of power.

It is not possible, however, to say that perfect justice is done. If the authoritarian characters suffer from a secret *malaise* and eventually come to grief, they nevertheless have their full stomachs and public dignity for compensation; revenge is sudden and therefore incomplete. The meek victims, by contrast, are in continual misery (if they survive at all) until the reversal occurs, and even then they retain their internalized sense of persecution. Hepzibah and Clifford, who are presented as figures of infantile innocence, are more pathetic in trying to enjoy their freedom after Jaffrey's death than in their former state of intimidation. "For, what other dungeon is so dark as one's own heart! What jailer so inexorable as one's self!" (III, 204) These sentences, applied to two characters who have done nothing wrong and indeed have been virtually incapable of feeling temptation, may remind us that Hawthorne's focus is not on moral guilt but on a broader phenomenon of psychological tyranny. The very prominence of Hepzibah and Clifford in the plot, along with the somewhat ponderous emphasis on the wasting-away of the Pyncheon energies from generation to generation, suggests that impotence rather than guilt may be Hawthorne's true theme.

I mean the term *impotence* in both a social and sexual sense. It is implied that in some way the Pyncheons have become effete by continuing to deny the claims of the vigorous and plebeian Maules. We could say that a failure of adaptation to modern democratic conditions has left the Pyncheons socially and economically powerless. Clearly, however, this failure has a sexual dimension. Not the least of the Maules' secret privileges is to "haunt . . . the chambers into which future bridegrooms were to lead their brides" (III, 21f.)—a fairly direct reference to some interference with normal sexuality. Just as denial of the earthy Maule element in society leads eventually to a loss of social power, so the same denial in emotional nature—symbolized by refusal to intermarry with the Maule line—leads to a loss of sexual power. Hepzibah and Clifford are the embodied result of these denials, as we shall see.

The conjunction of the sexual and social themes is best illustrated in Holgrave's legend of Alice Pyncheon. The aristocratic Alice, who "deemed herself conscious of a power—combined of beauty, high, unsullied purity, and the preservative force of womanhood—that could make her sphere impenetrable" (III, 242), is in effect seduced by the second Matthew Maule. The language of the entire episode is transparently sexual, and Alice is drawn not merely by mesmeric prowess but by "the remarkable comeliness, strength, and energy of Maule's figure" (III, 240). The outcome of this seduction, however, is not a union of any sort. Having been socially insulted by Alice's arrogant father, Maule uses his sexual mastery only to demonstrate sadistic control over Alice. "A power that she little dreamed of had laid its grasp upon her maiden soul. A will, most unlike her own, constrained her to do its grotesque and fantastic bidding." (III, 249)

This is to say that Maule is perversely toying with Alice's unladylike susceptibility to his erotic appeal, much as the other Maules exploit the Pyncheons' unpaid debt to them. The purpose is exactly opposite to healthy fulfillment, as the final event of Alice's life makes especially clear. The still-virginal Alice, who "would have deemed it sin to marry" because she is "so lost from self-control" (III, 250), is hypnotically summoned to attend Matthew Maule's wedding to a laborer's daughter. Alice's former "purity" and her class-consciousness—they are really a single fastidiousness—are thus successfully flouted; she is spurned and mocked by a man who supposedly had no claim on her interest. Significantly, the only "penetration" of Alice's "sphere" occurs on the way home from this wedding, when a fatal dose of consumption makes its entry into "her thinly sheltered bosom" (III, 250). Alice becomes a romantic prototype of the latter, more realistically inhibited Pyncheons who find themselves removed from the possibility of sexual fulfillment. The warfare between repression and the repressed will end only with the marriage of a Pyncheon to a Maule, and this will occur only after the chief impediment to both social and sexual democracy is removed.

What is that impediment? In Alice Pyncheon's case it is a father who imposes his elite pretensions on her, prevents her from considering marriage to a workingman, and half-willingly barters her away for a greedy purpose of his own. Each detail recalls the peculiarly unhealthy situation of Beatrice Rappaccini. When we turn to the modern Pyncheon "children," Hepzibah and Clifford, we find that the role of Gervayse Pyncheon or Dr. Rappaccini is played by cousin Jaffrey. Jaffrey is after the very same document that Gervayse Pyncheon was, and he too has made a "child"—the childlike Clifford—pay for his own criminality. Most strikingly, Jaffrey has hoarded to himself the dwindling sum of Pyncheon eroticism. Though he is not completely immune to the family enervation (see III, 148f.), Jaffrey is still characterized by "a kind of fleshly effulgence" (III, 144) and by "brutish . . . animal instincts" (III, 368). In his hypocritical gesture of family affection toward Phoebe, "the man, the sex, somehow or other, was entirely too prominent . . ." (III, 146). And it is suggested more than once that Jaffrey, like his first Puritan ancestor, "had fallen into certain transgressions to which men of his great animal development, whatever their faith or principles, must continue liable . . ." (III, 151). We begin to understand that the theory of Pyncheon decline —a decline that seems to apply only to real or metaphorical children—is inseparable from the recurrence in each generation of a licentious and selfish male Pyncheon—a caricature of the Freudian child's imagined father.

Two lines of a familiar triangle are thus discernible as an underlying configuration in *The House of the Seven Gables:* an overbearing, terrifying, and guilty "father" is matched against innocent but emotionally withered "children." The third line, which we could infer equally well from Hawthorne's previous work or from psychoanalytic doctrine, should be incest fear—the fantasy-terror which goes into the very idea of an all-forbidding and self-indulging Jaffrey Pyncheon. The Oedipal villain, in other words, is an embodied idea of paternal punishment for thoughts of incest, and the form actually taken by such punishment is impotence.

As it happens, *The House of the Seven Gables* abounds in ambiguous innuendo about both incest and impotence. Thus, for example, Holgrave uses the Pyncheons to illustrate a caution against too prolonged a family dynasty: "in their brief New England pedigree, there has been time enough to infect them all with one kind of lunacy or another!" (III, 222) What cannot quite be uttered about human inbreeding can be said of the family chickens, who are explicit emblems of their owners (see III, 184): "It was evident that the race had degenerated, like many a noble race besides, in consequence of too strict a watchfulness to keep it pure" (III, 113). Whether incest has been literally committed is as open a question for the Pyncheons as it was for the Mannings (see p. 36f. above); the real significance of the incest hints lies in their connection to the other Oedipal features of the total work. Those features do not encourage us to look for evidence of actual incest, but on the contrary for the emotional starvation that ensues from a morbid dread of incest. And this is exactly what we find in the decrepit siblings, Hepzibah and Clifford.

Hepzibah is of course a classic old maid, and Hawthorne keeps the sexual implications of her state before our minds. He introduces her in mock-erotic terms ("Far from us be the indecorum of assisting, even in imagination, at a maiden lady's toilet!" [III, 46]), and he repeatedly characterizes her feelings as those of an aged virgin. He also supplies us with what might be an etiological suggestion as to why Hepzibah has remained virginal. Unlike the other modern Pyncheons, she willingly submits herself to the imposing portrait of the first Colonel Pyncheon: "She, in fact, felt a reverence for the pictured visage, of which only a far-descended and time-stricken virgin could be susceptible" (III, 50). The father of the Pyncheon dynasty has acquired some of the affection that would normally be reserved for a husband. And this admittedly dim suggestion of incestuous feeling is greatly heightened by Hepzibah's secret and tender absorption in another portrait, whose subject might well have been "an early lover of Miss Hepzibah" (III, 48)—but is in truth her brother Clifford as a young man!

Clifford in turn is effeminate and attached to the image of his mother. His physical traits alone are emphatically revealing: "full, tender lips, and beautiful eyes" (III, 48), a face "almost too soft and gentle for a man's" (III, 117), "thin delicate fingers" (III, 174), and so on. His portrait not only shows "feminine traits, moulded inseparably with those of the other sex"; it also makes one think inevitably "of the original as resembling his mother, and she a lovely and lovable woman, with perhaps some beautiful infirmity of character ..." (III, 80). And later we hear of Clifford's dreams, "in which he invariably played the part of a child, or a very young man. So vivid were they . . . that he once held a dispute with his sister as to the particular figure or print of a chintz morning-dress, which he had seen their mother wear, in the dream of the preceding night" (III, 205). Clifford's dream-memory turns out to be exact.

If Clifford's mother is his dream, I find it significant that Jaffrey, who is blamed for his passage directly "from a boy into an old and broken man" (III, 205), is called his "nightmare" (III, 299, 371). Here again the strictest Freudian expectations are fulfilled. The melodramatic villainy of the "father" is blamed for a failure of manhood whose sources are clearly temperamental, and which antedates that villainy. The power of intimidation which Jaffrey has come to symbolize is explained by the manner of Clifford's brief release from it at Jaffrey's death. In a wild exhilaration that contrasts sharply with Hepzibah's more anxious response, Clifford simultaneously tosses off Oedipal rivalry, the Puritan past, and moral restraint; they are all revealed to be emotionally identical. Rocketing to an unknown modern destination on a railroad train that is leaving Jaffrey's corpse ever farther behind, the timid eunuch Clifford suddenly becomes a universal Eros. By means of the telegraph, he predicts excitedly, "Lovers, day by day,—hour by hour, if so often moved to do it,—might send their heart-throbs from Maine to Florida, with some such words as these, 'I love you forever!'—'My heart runs over with love!'—'I love you more than I can!' and, again, at the next message, 'I have lived an hour longer, and love you twice as much!'" (III, 313). This is the Clifford who feared to venture outside his home while Jaffrey lived.

Clifford is perhaps the supreme example in Hawthorne's fiction of a man whose feelings have become polarized between an exquisite aestheticism and frustrated sensuality. His worship of the beautiful and his hypersensitivity are matched by his huge appetite for food and his rather prurient titillation in the company of the developing virgin, Phoebe. Though his interest in her is described as chaste, Hawthorne adds that

> He was a man, it is true, and recognized her as a woman. . . . He took unfailing note of every charm that appertained to her sex, and saw the ripeness of her lips, and the virginal development of her bosom. All her little womanly ways, budding out of her like blossoms on a young fruit-tree, had their effect on him, and sometimes caused his very heart to tingle with the keenest thrills of pleasure. At such moments,—for the effect was seldom more than momentary,—the half-torpid man would be full of harmonious life, just as a long-silent harp is full of sound, when the musician's fingers sweep across it. (III, 171f.)

Significantly, Phoebe's company enables Clifford to retreat more easily into a state of childhood (see III, 180)—one in which his "gentle and voluptuous emotion" (III, 48) need meet no challenges from mature sexual reality.

To understand why Phoebe produces just this effect on Clifford, it is now necessary to consider her general symbolic role in the romance. It is, of course, a redemptive role, though by no means a theological one. To the social and psychological decadence of the House she brings one supreme virtue that has thus far been lacking: "There was no morbidness in Phoebe" (III, 166). Her function is to dispense symbolic sunshine (note her name) where hereditary gloom prevailed before. This is very obvious; but as always in Hawthorne's serious work, the banal theme is rooted in psychological relationships of considerable subtlety.

On the patent level Phoebe represents a kind of innocent energy and prettiness, a domestic competence unhindered by any brooding over the meaning of things. Her Pyncheon blood endows her marriage to Holgrave-Maule with familial symbolism, but in fact she is antithetical to most of the Pyncheon traits, and her effect on the ancestral property is to cancel or reverse many of its dark implications. Thus in the Pyncheon garden, "unctuous with nearly two hundred years of vegetable decay" (III, 93), she discovers a perfect rose, with "not a speck of blight or mildew in it" (III, 137). This "nice girl" and "cheerful little body" (III, 96, 97) aligns herself with all the symbols of persisting purity amid the general collapse—with the singing birds and above all with the unpolluted fountain in the garden. She is even able to neutralize the suggestive implications of her very bedroom, where "the joy of bridal nights had throbbed itself away." Hawthorne assures us that "a person of delicate instinct would have known at once that it was now a maiden's bedchamber, and had been purified of all former evil and sorrow by her sweet breath and happy thoughts. Her dreams of the past night, being such cheerful ones, had exorcised the gloom, and now haunted the chamber in its stead" (III, 95).

Now, this passage shows us Phoebe's chief part in the romance, which is not simply to stand for innocence but to refute or "exorcise" sexual cynicism. Hepzibah and Clifford, after all, are innocent enough; but Phoebe's purity has thematic weight because she is seen at the brink of womanhood. Hawthorne deliberately puts her within a sexual perspective in order to declare her exempt from erotic inclinations. She dreams, but cheerfully; she has "brisk impulses" (III, 209), but they urge her to hike in the countryside; her "ordinary little toils," unlike Hester Prynne's, do not register unfulfilled desire but merely "perfect health" (III, 167). She is even observed by Clifford at the moment of recognizing the existence of her emergent sexual appeal, yet she pays for this recognition with nothing more than a maidenly blush and a slight modification of her forthrightness (see III, 263).

Phoebe's role is epitomized at one point in a striking oxymoron. In neutralizing the morbidity of her surroundings she is said to wield a "homely witchcraft" (III, 94)—that is, a marriage of spiritual power and tidy domesticity. In Hawthorne's usual world this is unthinkable; one can be either a conventional nobody or a moral outlaw with a special potency of spirit. The "limit-loving" (III, 161) Phoebe, in contrast, derives her power of exorcism precisely from her ignorant conventionality—indeed, from her unwillingness to face unpleasant truths. This is especially apparent in her relations with Clifford: "whatever was morbid in his mind and experience she ignored; and thereby kept their intercourse healthy . . ." (III, 173). So, too, she innocently evades the lecherous Jaffrey's kiss (see III, 145) and fails to confirm Hepzibah's original fears that she will be a rival for Clifford's love (see III, 91, 98). When she finally confesses that her sentiments toward Hepzibah and Clifford have been maternal (see III, 258), this exemption from sexuality takes on an Oedipal significance. Despite her youth Phoebe stands in the place of an ideal parent, a selfless breadwinner and moral guide who can replace the tyrannical parent of guilty fantasy.

The real test of this role is provided by Holgrave, whose interest in Phoebe is necessarily amorous. Like Jaffrey, he is both haunting and haunted. As a Maule he owns the mesmeric power which seduces and destroys, yet this power leaves him prone to self-destructive monomania. By marrying Phoebe after virtually hypnotizing her and then allowing her to go free after all, he offers a model of self-restraint from the morbid "experimentation" upon womankind that is so tempting for Hawthornian males generally. He and Phoebe together—he having renounced his unconscious, she scarcely having noticed hers—finally embody a contradictory but necessary vision of mature love combined with indefinitely protracted childhood.

It is noteworthy that Hawthorne strains verisimilitude in order to work Holgrave into his concern for fathers and sons. Without any apparent reason the resourceful and independent daguerreotypist is oppressed by the figure of Jaffrey Pyncheon in death. As he tells Phoebe,

> "The presence of yonder dead man threw a great black shadow over everything; he made the universe, so far as my perception could reach, a scene of guilt and of retribution more dreadful than the guilt. The sense of it took away my youth. I never hoped to feel young again! The world looked strange, wild, evil, hostile; my past life, so lonesome and dreary; my future, a shapeless gloom, which I must mould into gloomy shapes! But, Phoebe, you crossed the threshold; and hope, warmth, and joy came in with you!"
> (III, 362)

Here the theme of patricidal guilt, again as in "Roger Malvin's Burial," is being stretched to include a wholly symbolic father who has not been murdered at all. Holgrave's fear of "retribution" has no basis in stated motives, yet it reminds us that his view of society and history has been metaphorically Oedipal. The cruel world in his estimate is "that gray-bearded and wrinkled profligate, decrepit, without being venerable" (III, 215); and the tyranny of the past is "just as if a young giant were compelled to waste all his strength in carrying about the corpse of the old giant, his grandfather, who died a long while ago, and only needs to be decently buried" (III, 219). Jaffrey's death thus satisfies a patricidal strain in Holgrave's nature—a fact which is corroborated by his "unmotivated" anxiety before Jaffrey's corpse.

The best indication that the "happy" outcome of *The House of the Seven Gables* was not cathartic for its contriver is an omnipresent uneasiness about the propriety, the honesty, and the quality of fictive art. From the defensively humble Preface onward Hawthorne seems to despair of sustaining the picturesque effects which he simultaneously equates with artistic value and denigrates as trickery. The ending to his plot confirms his pessimism: modern ordinariness triumphs over a compulsive and romantic addiction to the past. To a certain extent this pattern is put to good comic use; in the world of homely witchcraft the only ghosts are "the ghosts of departed cook-maids" (III, 124), and Maule's well is no more bewitched than "an old lady's cup of tea" (III, 120). Especially in his treatment of Hepzibah, who resembles him in trying to sell to "a different set of customers" such traditional wares as "sugar figures, with no strong resemblance to the humanity of any epoch . . ." (III, 53), Hawthorne manages to take a whimsical view of his artistic plight. Like her creator in his post-college years, Hepzibah, "by secluding herself from society, has lost all true relation with it" (III, 257f.) and must now try to "flash forth on the world's astonished gaze at once" (III, 57). And yet her failure to do so—her bondage to an anachronistic stock-in-trade—has a desperate autobiographical meaning for Hawthorne. He as well as Hepzibah, if they are to stay in business at all, must follow the cynical advice on modern salesmanship offered by the earthbound Yankee, Uncle Venner: "Put on a bright face for your customers, and smile pleasantly as you hand them what they ask for! A stale article, if you dip it in a good, warm, sunny smile, will go off better than a fresh one that you've scowled upon" (III, 87).[5]

---

[5] The Hawthorne-Hepzibah parallel can be carried further. In her devotion to the past Hepzibah is said by Holgrave to be "peopling the world with ugly shapes, which you will soon find to be as unreal as the giants and ogres

If Hepzibah illustrates the futility of Hawthornian art in the nineteenth century, Clifford and Holgrave may be said to illustrate the flaws and dangers of the artistic temperament. Clifford, the artist *manqué*, is both squeamish and vicariously sensual, both "ideal" and secretly voracious. At times he is merely irritable and dull, but occasionally his fantasy is given symbolic rein, as when he blows artistic bubbles to be pricked by unappreciative passersby (see III, 206f.). In either capacity, however, he remains enveloped in a robe of moonshine, "which he hugged about his person, and seldom let realities pierce through" (III, 205). Thus he is an extreme version of the withdrawn Hawthornian artist, and it is not difficult to see what he has withdrawn from. His "images of women," says Hawthorne, "had more and more lost their warmth and substance, and been frozen, like the pictures of secluded artists, into the chillest ideality" (III, 170). As usual, ideality and coldness toward women are the same thing, and are associated with "secluded artists." Only Phoebe, the embodied negation of all unpleasant fantasies about women, can persuade Clifford that "the world was no longer a delusion."[6]

Similarly, Phoebe aids Holgrave in restraining his tendency to be an "all-observant" (III, 189) peeper. His interest in his companions has essentially been an author's overview of his characters, and at one point he actually makes a literary work out of Pyncheon history. Alice Pyncheon's legend and the circumstances of its narration sum up everything Hawthorne has to say about the

---

of a child's story-book" (III, 62). The prediction comes true: Hepzibah and Clifford eventually "bade a final farewell to the abode of their forefathers, with hardly more emotion than if they had made it their arrangement to return thither at tea-time" (III, 377). While this is pleasant for Hepzibah, from Hawthorne's point of view it is entirely too easy. He is committed as an artist to the realm of picturesque ancestral guilt which even Hepzibah finds outdated and indeed imaginary.

[6] One of Hawthorne's miniature allegories of art is especially revealing in this connection. Clifford finds himself aesthetically delighted by an organ-grinder's puppets, until he notices the lewd and greedy monkey who is collecting coins. He is especially struck by the monkey's "wrinkled and abominable little visage" and his "thick tail curling out into preposterous prolixity from beneath his tartans" (III, 197). This tail, "too enormous to be decently concealed," betokens a "deviltry of nature" that is particularly offensive to Clifford-as-artist; for the monkey is seizing pennies on behalf of a parody of art. Clifford "had taken childish delight in the music, and smiled, too, at the figures which it set in motion. But, after looking a while at the long-tailed imp, he was so shocked by his horrible ugliness, spiritual as well as physical, that he actually began to shed tears . . ." (III, 198). Clifford weeps for his own secret feeling that the aesthetic realm is polluted by greed and lust.

secret meaning of art. The legend itself, says Holgrave, "has taken hold of my mind with the strangest tenacity of clutch . . ." and he is telling it "as one method of throwing it off" (III, 223). Authorship, including the intention to publish the work in a magazine, is presented as a way of mastering obsession. Yet Holgrave has a more immediate purpose as well, to impress Phoebe with his talent. The covert eroticism of the story is evidently communicated to its listener, for at the end she "leaned slightly towards [Holgrave], and seemed almost to regulate her breath by his":

> A veil was beginning to be muffled about her, in which she could behold only him, and live only in his thoughts and emotions. His glance, as he fastened it on the young girl, grew involuntarily more concentrated; in his attitude there was the consciousness of power, investing his hardly mature figure with a dignity that did not belong to its physical manifestation. It was evident that, with but one wave of his hand and a corresponding effort of his will, he could complete his mastery over Phoebe's yet free and virgin spirit: he could establish an influence over this good, pure, and simple child, as dangerous, and perhaps as disastrous, as that which the carpenter of his legend had acquired and exercised over the ill-fated Alice. (III, 252f.)

The thinly euphemistic nature of this scene presumably enabled its first readers to ignore, or at least to perceive indistinctly, the implication that cheery little Phoebe is endowed with sexual desire. She unconsciously welcomes her seducer, and he "involuntarily" tightens his hold on her. This hold has been won through the mesmeric power of art, and motivated not simply by desire but by the prying and rapacious tendency which in Hawthorne's harsh view constitutes the artistic character. That tendency must be "cured," at least in symbolism, if a satisfactory resolution is to be reached. And thus Holgrave obligingly steps out of his Maule identity and reforms both himself and the spirit of the romance. He relaxes his spell over Phoebe and allows her deliberate obtuseness to have the final say: "But for this short life of ours, one would like a house and a moderate garden-spot of one's own" (III, 188). At the end, though the revitalized Pyncheon chickens have begun "an indefatigable process of egg-laying" (III, 372), art has been tacitly set aside and forgotten.

The logic of this conclusion is impeccable. If the image of Jaffrey Pyncheon in death makes Holgrave's future appear to be "a shapeless gloom, which I must mould into gloomy shapes," and if Phoebe alone can erase that image from his mind, then marriage to Phoebe obviates the need for moulding further "gloomy shapes." To become free of anxiety is to lose all reason for creativity. For Holgrave it cannot matter that Phoebe is in fact a tissue of symbolic contradictions: motherly child, sisterly bride, fertile and prolific virgin. It is Hawthorne for whom this subtle compromise is finally meaningful. And in a broader sense the incongruities of his plot—the yoking together of ancestral guilt, of maladaptation to modern reality, and of a villain's death which produces unholy erotic glee and a therapeutic marriage—find their rationale in Hawthorne's struggle to disbelieve that the world is indeed "a scene of guilt and of retribution more dreadful than the guilt." Not Holgrave but Hawthorne, who called his wife Phoebe, has set Phoebe-ism as the steep ransom from obsession. And it is Hawthorne, ultimately, who with secret and wistful irony measures the consequence of this surrender for his own later career. "The world owes all its onward impulses to men ill at ease," he has Holgrave tell Phoebe with great truthfulness; and shortly thereafter Holgrave adds, "If we love one another, the moment has room for nothing more" (III, 363).

Henry Nash Smith

The House of the Seven Gables as Social History

The subversive threat of commercialism could wear a quite different aspect for an observer not supported by Cooper's aristocratic self-confidence or Emerson's metaphysical optimism. And Nathaniel Hawthorne had neither of these resources. In *The House of the Seven Gables*, published in 1851, he gives a central position to a character endowed with many of the traits that Emerson attributes to Napoleon, such as "hard, keen sense, and practical energy," an "immitigable resolve," and a "hot fellness of purpose, which annihilated everything but itself." Judge Jaffrey Pyncheon, says Hawthorne, was "powerful by intellect, energy of will, the long habit of acting among men": he was "bold, imperious, relentless, crafty; laying his purposes deep, and following them out with an inveteracy of pursuit that knew neither rest nor conscience; trampling on the weak, and, when essential to his ends, doing his utmost to beat down the strong." Since we actually see the Judge in action

---

From "The Morals of Power" in *Essays on American Literature in Honor of Jay B. Hubbell* edited by Clarence Gohdes (Durham, N.C.: Duke University Press, 1967), pp. 92-97. Reprinted by permission of the author and the publishers.

only within a very limited theater of operations—"a rusty wooden house" in a by-street of the town of Salem—his career lacks the epic grandeur of Napoleon's military campaigns on three continents. But the Judge's lust for money and power identifies him with the rising commercialism of which Emerson declares Napoleon to be the type.

The Judge's activities on the specimen day for which Hawthorne gives us a detailed program were to be primarily concerned with business matters. He would have spent some time in an insurance office exchanging gossip with men of financial influence; he was to preside at a meeting of bank directors; and later he was to meet "a State Street broker, who has undertaken to procure a heavy percentage, and the best of paper, for a few loose thousands which the Judge happens to have by him, uninvested." To be sure, these business activities are not developed with the documentary detail we have come to expect in realistic fiction. Hawthorne disdains them, and evidently conceives of them in terms of clichés. Of the bank directors' meeting, he remarks in scorn, "Let him go thither, and loll at ease upon his money-bags!" But the intention is to depict the Judge as being deeply involved in financial transactions.

Hawthorne places further emphasis on the lust for wealth as a force of evil in his references to the past. The "legend" presented in the romance, "prolonging itself, from an epoch now gray in the distance, down into our own broad daylight," begins with the crime of the founder of the family, the seventeenth-century Colonel Pyncheon who caused Matthew Maule to be executed for witchcraft so that he might seize Maule's property. The same ruthless greed has appeared in an eighteenth-century Pyncheon, and the pattern has been repeated once again in the early career of the nineteenth-century Judge. We are to understand that in his youth Jaffrey Pyncheon contrived to have his cousin Clifford sent to prison for thirty years for the alleged murder of a wealthy uncle who actually died of natural causes. The motive was Jaffrey's desire to secure for himself the inheritance originally destined for Clifford. At the climax of the plot of *The House of the Seven Gables*, Judge Pyncheon attempts to force the enfeebled Clifford to reveal to him the hiding place of certain documents that the Judge believes will enable him to lay claim to valuable lands "to the Eastward" acquired by the Pyncheon family at some remote point in the past. To this end he threatens to have Clifford, only recently released from prison, confined in an insane asylum; and he is prevented from executing his threat only by a mysterious stroke which kills him as he sits waiting for an interview with Clifford in the old family mansion.

This material is essentially melodramatic; it has the stereotyped air of popular "sensation fiction." Not only are the crimes ascribed to Judge Pyncheon so outrageous as to be unbelievable; Hawthorne makes no effort to provide a plausible motivation for the character's behavior, and seems to be concerned only with making him a totally repulsive villain. Hawthorne's undisguised hatred rises to a climax in the remarkable chapter called "Governor Pyncheon." The only actual character on stage is the Judge, and he is dead: his corpse sits upright in a great oaken armchair. No action is performed and no word spoken by anyone except the author, who is so completely mastered by a savage, Old Testament exultation that he devotes pages on end to taunting his dead enemy and even executes a kind of verbal dance of triumph around the corpse.

Hawthorne's portrayal of Judge Pyncheon is too strongly colored by emotion to be accepted as merely an abstract denunciation of greed. Cooper, for example, evidently disliked commercialism as much as Hawthorne did. Yet there is nothing in Cooper's treatment of this theme that even approaches the intensity of Hawthorne's feeling toward Jaffrey Pyncheon. A significant difference is the element of fear in Hawthorne's attitude. To be sure, he says that Clifford might have been able to withstand the shock of contemplating unbridled greed, "the worst and meanest aspect of life," if he had had a tragic power of scornful laughter. And there are moments of grim comedy in Hawthorne's taunting of the Judge's corpse. But the basic emotion of the chapter is more accurately expressed in his exclamation toward the end: "Yonder leaden Judge sits immovably upon our soul. Will he never stir again? We shall go mad unless he stirs!"

Frederick Crews proposes to read *The House of the Seven Gables* as an act of exorcism in which the Judge, as a father figure, must be destroyed in accord with the imperatives of an Oedipal pattern. This view seems to me persuasive. It accounts not only for the intensity of Hawthorne's feeling, but for the elaborate symbolism with which he surrounds the Judge's death, such as the sudden appearance of a Golden Bough in the Pyncheon Elm, and the unexpected blooming of flowers among the plants growing in roof angles of the old house. Most important of all, Mr. Crews's interpretation makes sense of the whole peripeteia of the fable, the release of vital energies in all the surviving characters and the declaration of love between Holgrave and Phoebe that provides a comic resolution for the plot.

The Freudian view can readily accommodate the economic and in the broad sense political meanings that I have pointed to in the characterization of Judge Pyncheon. Even if we do not wish to go so far as to note that money often stands for libido in Freudian constructions, we can recognize that Hawthorne links the Judge's relentless drive to amass wealth with sexual tyranny. The close association between the two themes appears with especial clarity in one of the most fully worked out emblematic episodes in the book. An Italian with a barrel-organ and a monkey stops in the street under the windows of the old house. While he turns the crank, the monkey capers about, begging coins from the onlookers. Hawthorne moralizes the scene with emphasis:

> The mean and low, yet strangely man-like expression of his wilted countenance; the prying and crafty glance, that showed him to be ready to gripe at every miserable advantage; his enormous tail (too enormous to be decently concealed under his gabardine), and the deviltry of nature which it betokened,—take this monkey just as he was, in short, and you could desire no better image of the Mammon of copper coin, symbolizing the grossest form of the love of money.

In this passage, as elsewhere in the story, Hawthorne associates a voracious love of money with suggestions of gross sexuality: the monkey's deviltry is evident both in his greedy snatching of coins and in the repulsively phallic tail. Mr. Crews notes a number of references to Judge Pyncheon's "fleshly effulgence," his "great animal development"; and Hawthorne also hints darkly at outrageous sexual behavior that hastened the death of his wife. The overt indictment of the Judge as a man dominated by a craving for wealth gains force from the partly explicit sexual symbolism. The author's hostility toward a single character tends to become a repudiation of all forms of established authority.

It must be added, however, that this subversive emotion finds only indirect and muffled expression: the force of inhibition is too strong. Although Holgrave is the most formidable adversary of the Judge, Hawthorne does not manage to bring them face to face in open conflict. Instead, Holgrave is represented as being an economic and political radical. He cherishes rather vague doctrines about the need to tear down "the moss-grown and rotten Past" so that a golden era may be inaugurated for mankind. Like Hawthorne, he has even "spent some months in a community of Fourierists"; and Hawthorne expresses a considerable sympathy for Holgrave's "enthusiasm" in the very act of declaring it to be a "crude, wild, and misty philosophy." It is true that the young man renounces his radicalism in order to marry Phoebe and take possession of the Judge's inheritance, but there is a certain hangdog air about his recantation, and the conclusion of the story is notably lacking in imaginative power.

For our purposes, the most significant aspect of the implied antagonism between Judge Pyncheon and Holgrave is Hawthorne's identification of commercialism and wealth with official status in the community. Business interests are already in control of society. The young man, the archetypal son who is hostile to the Establishment, is indifferent to the profit motive. This pattern contradicts Emerson's conception, which associates "the spirit of commerce, of money and material power" with "the democratic classes," "the young and the poor who have fortunes to make" and are "recruiting their numbers every hour by births," and opposes this group to the "idle capitalists"—a class that is "continually losing numbers by death." With some forcing of the issue, we might say that Emerson regards the typical businessman as being self-made, like Napoleon, whereas in using Jaffrey Pyncheon to represent the commercial spirit Hawthorne moves toward the Jacksonian contention that the business system was an aristocratic money power hostile to the plain people.

This would perhaps be an oversimplification of Hawthorne's complex vision of his materials. Nevertheless, on one point Hawthorne is quite clear and recognizably Jacksonian. Judge Pyncheon is a Whig (he even has a few traits suggesting Daniel Webster) and he is eager to continue his political career as the corrupt servant of conservative economic interests. Hawthorne tells us that on the day he did not live to see, the Judge was supposed to attend a dinner,

> the most important, in its consequences, of all the dinners [he] ever ate! The guests were to be some dozen or so friends from several districts of the State; men of distinguished character and influence . . . practised politicians, every man of them, and skilled to adjust those preliminary measures which steal from the people, without its knowledge, the power of choosing its own rulers. The popular voice, at the next gubernatorial election, though loud as thunder, will be really an echo of what those gentlemen shall

speak, under their breath, at your friend's festive board. They meet to decide upon their candidate. This little knot of subtle schemers will control the convention, and, through it, dictate to the party. And what worthier candidate,—more wise and learned, more noted for philanthropic liberality, truer to safe principles, tried oftener by public trusts, more spotless in private character, with a larger stake in the common welfare, and deeper grounded, by hereditary descent, in the faith and character of the Puritans,—what man can be presented for the suffrage of the people, so eminently combining all these claims to the chief-rulership as Judge Pyncheon here before us?

In this parody of a nominating speech at a political convention we can feel the weight of experience in a writer who had held a patronage appointment as a "Loco-Foco Surveyor" in the Salem Customs House, and would presently write a campaign biography of his college classmate and friend Franklin Pierce. Hawthorne knew what he was talking about when he urged the Judge, "Be present at this dinner!—drink a glass or two of that noble wine!—make your pledges in as low a whisper as you will!—and you rise up from table virtually governor of the glorious old State! Governor Pyncheon of Massachusetts!"

The ironic allusions to "safe principles" and to the stake-in-society theory of politics are an attack on the conception of government as an instrument of the wealthiest men. The pledges that the Judge would have made in return for the nomination are left ominously vague, but their general nature can be inferred. When he fails to appear at the dinner, the diners are unperturbed; they are "warm and merry; they have given up the Judge; and, concluding that the Free-Soilers have him, they will fix upon another candidate." The actual man in office is a matter of indifference, since the real control is exercised by business interests behind the scenes.

Edward C. Sampson

Some Sights and Sounds

It is possible to group or classify some of the specific details that Hawthorne uses: details that involve light and shadow, nature, the house, and sounds; it will be helpful to look at some of these more closely.

When Hawthorne speaks of his story as a "legend prolonging itself, from an epoch now gray in the distance, down into our own broad daylight," he suggests something of the symbolic meaning of darkness and light. Phoebe's very name associates her with light, and the sun, as well as with birds and nature; darkness is frequently associated with Judge Pyncheon (when the true nature of the man shows forth), and reaches a climax in the "Governor Pyncheon" chapter. Hawthorne does not use light and shadow as insistently as he does in *The Scarlet Letter*—Judge Pyncheon is not quite a Chillingworth—but in a general way, light and dark, sunshine and shadow, suggest the true and the false, the good and the bad, the bright present and the gloomy past. Phoebe's natural

---

Extracts from an afterword to *The House of the Seven Gables,* A Signet Classic, published by the New American Library, New York and Toronto, 1961, pp. 281-283 + 286. Reprinted with the permission of the author.

goodness is highlighted by the sunshine she brings with her; the burden of the past is represented, in part, by the darkness of the House of the Seven Gables (originally, the glittering plaster of the house had been prominent); and darkness has clouded most of Hepzibah's life. The final removal of Clifford and Hepzibah from the old house brings them, we suppose, what light remains in their lives: Hepzibah says of Clifford, "He has had but little sunshine in his life . . . and, oh, what a black shadow!"

   A multitude of specific details in the novel involve nature: they form one of the chief imagery patterns, and are handled with as much sureness as is the nature imagery in *The Scarlet Letter*. The house, for example, is associated in some ways with nature—strikingly so when "Alice's Posies" bloom after the storm. When Holgrave and Phoebe work in the garden, we can see them not simply as the new generation, but as a modern Adam and Eve—a view that is strengthened when Holgrave suggests a division of labor in the garden tasks that reminds us of the division of labor that Eve proposes to Adam in *Paradise Lost*. The effect of all the nature references is to emphasize the influence of Phoebe on the lives of Hepzibah, Clifford, and Holgrave. As the pleasant aspects of nature are in opposition to the weeds and burdocks, to the moss and dry rot, so Phoebe works to overcome the dark shadow of the past that has blighted the lives of Clifford and Hepzibah. The flowering of the posies is indeed an "expression that something within the house was consummated"—not only the death of the Judge, but the triumph of the present, and of good, over the curse of the past. The house itself, a symbol of the past, is almost taken over by the elm and the plants, as Hawthorne points out the natural antagonism of nature toward man's attempts to preserve that past.

   Hawthorne makes frequent reference to the various parts of the house. So clear, indeed, is his picture that in spite of his warning in the Preface, some people claim to see the original in one of the old houses in Salem. One word in particular—"threshold"—though unimportant in itself, is used with more than the expected frequency, and serves as a clue to an important aspect of the story. Hawthorne speaks of being himself at the "threshold of our story"; Hepzibah, Uncle Venner tells us, used to sit as a child at the threshold of the house; Phoebe, when she comes to the house, stands at the threshold; and Clifford, when he first appears to Phoebe, pauses long at the threshold. The particular detail becomes symbolic: Hepzibah and Clifford are at the threshold of the outside world, and they make the transition for good at the end.

Phoebe, a young girl, is on the threshold of womanhood. With the maturity she gains from living in the house, and with her acceptance of Holgrave's love, she, too, moves to a new point in life—"less girlish, but more a woman." Holgrave turns away from his over-ambitious ideas of reform; the Judge crosses the threshold from life to death; and even Uncle Venner enters, in his old age, into a new and unexpected security. What is emphasized here is the chief movement of the plot, which is not so much a matter of withdrawal and return, as H. H. Waggoner has suggested, but a series of movements away from a previous condition to a new and happier one.

Critics have noted other interesting groups of details: Hawthorne's use of "substance and shadow" words; his suggestions that the house is a living being; and his use of circle and sphere images. Scarcely commented on, however, is his frequent use of sound in the story. In *The Scarlet Letter*, the sound that one is apt to remember is Dimmesdale's midnight shriek. In *The House of the Seven Gables*, the sounds are many, some unpleasant, but most pleasant. Perhaps Henry James was thinking of the sounds when he spoke of the story as having a charm "like that of the sweetness of a piece of music," or, he adds later, "that vague hum, that indefinable echo, of the whole multitudinous life of man, which is the real sign of a great work of fiction." We remember the clamor of the shop bell—harsher to Hepzibah's ears than to Phoebe's—and the choking gurgle of the victims of Maule's curse. But we also remember the pleasant sound of the hurdy-gurdy, the noise of the scissor-grinder's wheel, the "blessed sounds" of the church bells, the murmur of the bees in the garden, and the singing locusts in the elm tree. Clifford is first presented as a voice; and at the end, the almost celestial music of Alice Pyncheon's harpsichord is more real, more convincing, as well as more meaningful, because of all the sounds that have gone before.

But what of Clifford? If he is in fact the main character, how does he figure in the theme? The answer is that the theme, as tentatively stated a moment ago, needs modification. For, in spite of the apparently happy ending of the story, the fact remains that the evil deeds of the past have not, in truth, been fully redeemed. Surely Woodberry was wrong when he said of Clifford that "one sees in him only the victim of life, the prisoner whom the law mistook and outraged." Why *only*, one asks? For in Clifford's life lies Hawthorne's final point: there are people who are born to be apart from the world, or to be wronged by it, and it is one of the tragedies of life that their problems have no solution, and that their suffering must be endured. Clifford, like the much stronger Jude, in Hardy's *Jude the Obscure*, cannot become a part of the life around him, and for the wrong he has suffered there is, as Hawthorne says, "no reparation. . . . No great mistake, whether acted or endured, in our mortal sphere, is ever really set right." The best Clifford can have, and Hawthorne mercifully gives it to him (as he had not given it to Hester in *The Scarlet Letter*), is a quiet contentment that is delicately balanced, and is scarcely more substantial than the soap bubbles that Clifford had blown from the balcony window of the House of the Seven Gables.

Klaus Lubbers

Metaphorical Patterns

With Hawthorne's fiction, it is more than usually tempting and misleading to discuss the conceptual framework before attending to what should precede such considerations—the study of his language. Nevertheless, characters and plots, structures, themes, and ideas have traditionally proved more attractive than the medium through which he informed them. Tongue in cheek, Hawthorne warns the reader in his preface to *The House of the Seven Gables* and, by the same token, challenges him to probe deeper: "When romances do really teach anything, or produce any effective operation, it is usually through a far more subtle process than the ostensible one" (4). One of the more obvious though largely neglected approaches to the core of the work would be the study of its imagery. The existence of such images as circles and squares, light and dark, colors and mirrors has regularly and dutifully been registered by critics, but its importance has consistently been

---

"Metaphorical Patterns in Hawthorne's *The House of the Seven Gables*" in *Literatur und Sprache der Vereinigten Staaten,* Essays in Honor of Hans Galinsky, ed. by Hans Helmcke, Klaus Lubbers and Renate Schmidt-v. Bardeleben (Heidelberg; Carl Winter—Universitätsverlag, 1969), pp. 107-116. Reprinted by permission of the author and the publisher.

underrated. How could we otherwise account for the fact that the function of lines and circles only has so far been adequately studied?

What follows is a far from complete continuation along this line: an analysis of the ways in which a number of prominent verbal patterns and metaphorical chains—"rusty," "venerable," "patched," "sphere," the mutual impregnation of the animate and the inanimate as well as the metaphors of the jail, the stream of life, and the world as theatre—contribute to the textural richness of *The House of the Seven Gables*. This analysis is offered not as an interpretation but rather as a prolegomenon to one.

I

"Rusty" was one of the epithets that stuck in Henry James's mind when he wrote about Hawthorne's romance. Along with the related substantives "rust" and "rustiness," it occurs twenty-one times with diminishing frequency (four times each in chapters I and II, twice each in chapters III, IV, and V). It is first said figuratively of the house, denoting old age and shabbiness. The metaphorical proliferation is interesting: six references are to the house, six to objects in it, four to Hepzibah's clothes, two to her person, and one each to the hens, to Uncle Venner, and to a nail found by an old man in the street. The arrangement of the links in the chain is as follows. In chapter I, "rusty" is applied exclusively to the mansion (9 "a rusty, wooden house"; 13 "its rusty old-age"; 22 "the rustiness and infirmity of age"; 28 "this desolate, decaying, gusty, rusty, old house of the Pyncheon family"). The next four references, in chapter II, alternate between the scales in the cent-shop and Hepzibah (34 the "rust" on the "brown scales"; 36 "her rigid and rusty frame"; 37 "the rusty scales"; 39 "a gaunt, sallow, rusty-jointed maiden"). From this point on, the designation, both in its original ('coated with rust') and transferred senses ('faded, old, shabby') assumes increasing mobility. It is used of the heroine's dress, "a gown of rusty black silk" (III, 46), of the shop door creaking on its "rusty hinges" (III, 46), of "the dilapidated and rusty-visaged House of the Seven Gables" (IV, 52), the "rusty key" of its portal (IV, 63) and "all its rusty old appliances" (V, 69), again of Hepzibah's "rustling and rusty silks" (V, 73), of the "queer, rusty, withered aspect" of the Pyncheon hens (VI, 79), the maiden's "rusty silks" (IX, 116), Uncle Venner's "rusty beaver" (XIV, 190), Hepzibah's "rusty black silk-gown" (XV, 192), a forlorn figure "in quest of rusty nails" (XVII, 218), the family home as it lives on as "rusty, crazy, creaky, dry-rotted, damp-rotted, dingy, dark, and miserable old dungeon" in Clifford's mind during his wild train ride (XVII, 224) and, in the last chapter, of a secret spring "eaten through with rust" (XXI, 217)—the very spring that had hidden the coveted parchment, the family's claim to boundless wealth in Waldo County, Maine. The movement of the metaphor starts out from the house and circles back to it in the end.

"Rusty" ("rust," "rustiness"), a key word indicative of the rotten past, of disuse, inactivity, and sterility, forms an associational cluster both inclusive and exclusive. Most strongly, it aligns the house (altogether twelve references) with one of its inmates (six references—Clifford, Phoebe, and Holgrave are excepted); less strongly, it attracts the hereditary garden fowls and old Venner (by his hat, not by his person). Significantly, the old man looking for nails is encountered by the two "owls" in a deserted street during their flight. It is instructive to see that the metaphor is used most frequently at the beginning of the novel and that its symbolic value is spelled out in the last reference which points to the pride and the avarice of the Pyncheons.

This selective concatenation of figures and objects may appear accidental. Yet Hawthorne deliberately drew together what he intended to be associated. "Lugubrious," an inconspicuous adjective occurring only in three places, is a case in point. It joins Hepzibah, the house, and the hens. On the first morning, we hear the maiden heaving "heavy sighs that labored from her bosom, with little restraint as to their lugubrious depth and volume of sound" (II, 30). On the second morning, we watch her giving Phoebe a tour of the house and "recounting the traditions with which, as we may say, the walls were lugubriously frescoed" (V, 74–75). That same evening, the niece visits the fowls in the hen coop and notices their "lugubrious deportment" (VI, 79). At this point the author drops the Latinism expressive of the dismal and the doleful.

More important is the role played by "venerable" which, like "rusty," refers to what is old but implies dignity instead of shabbiness and thus partly counterbalances "rusty." More restricted than the latter (it occurs fifteen times), this adjective performs a similar function and passes through a similar circular development. In chapter I, it is three times applied to the house (9 "the venerable mansion"; 22 "the venerable house"; 27 "its venerable peaks") and once to the "venerable beards" of the late seventeenth-century clergymen who crossed its threshold at the invitation of its first owner (15). Next, we find it employed to characterize Uncle Venner—which seems the less surprising as the first syllables of both adjective and family name are homophonous (IV, 56 "the venerable man"; IV, 59 "her venerable friend's look and tone"; V, 74 "the venerable man"). Although Hepzibah does not qualify for the designation, the chickens do (VI, 80 "The chicken . . . almost as venerable in appearance as its mother" and " 'Those venerable personages in the coop' "). The epithet then reverts to "the venerable Uncle Venner" (X, 134), to the puniest of the fowls, "the venerable chicken" (XIV, 189) and progresses to retired sea captains, "venerable quidnuncs" (XVII, 218), who witness the flight of brother and sister, and to the "venerably black" farm house which marks the farthest point the odd pair reach in their flight (XVII, 228). As with "rusty," the last two references are to the "venerable" House of the Seven Gables (XVIII, 230; XIX, 245).

Walter Allen, writing of Anne Radcliffe's novels of horror, sees in *The Mysteries of Udolpho* the first instance of a distinguished literary type characterized

> by a peculiarly intense relationship between the characters and their immediate environments. Character and environment are impregnated each with the other. To some extent environment is, as it were, humanized, and the character himself is as he is because of the environment and cannot be detached from it.

Hawthorne, himself much impressed by the Gothic genre from his youth, may have taken a cue from "The Fall of the House of Usher," the most intricate and uncanny example of the interfusing of character and ambience. At any rate, there is ample evidence of this mutual impregnation which one hesitates to deplore, with Philip Young, as mere trappings. Trappings there certainly are, but at least part of what is generally dismissed as Gothic embellishments would seem to be functional. The idea of the animated mansion is entrenched as early as chapter I. The author's stylistic device is comparison which only at times congeals into metaphor. In the second paragraph of the novel, the storyteller is "affected" by the house as by "a human countenance" (9). The projection of the second storey over the first "gave the house a meditative look"

(I, 27). It is "rusty-visaged" (IV, 52). The "battered visage" it shows to the world, usually "black and heavy-browed" (V, 73)— scowling with its arched windows like shortsighted Hepzibah?—is capable of facial change depending on the cheerfulness or gloominess of its inmates. Twice the countenance lights up under the influence of women in it but not of it. As Phoebe passes to and fro inside, it evinces "a kind of cheerfulness glimmering through its dusky windows" (V, 73). When Matthew Maule visits Gervayse Pyncheon in Holgrave's legend, it likewise "had that pleasant aspect of life, which is like the cheery expression of comfortable activity, in the human countenance" (XIII, 165). The bustle is caused by the large family, including sweet Alice, within. Behind its façade beats a heart synchronous with the Pyncheon past. "So much of mankind's varied experience had passed there . . . that the very timbers were oozy, as with the moisture of a heart. It was itself like a great human heart, with a life of its own" (I, 27; cf. XIX, 253). Later, the heart is emblematically identified with the fireplace (XV, 193). Small wonder, then, that the animated timber structure "sighs" (I, 17), "shivers" in the five-day easterly gale (XV, 193), and eructates through its throat (I, 14 "The chimney . . . belching forth its kitchen-smoke"; XV, 193 "the storm-demon kept watch above . . . choking the chimney's sooty throat with its own breath"; XVIII, 238 "a vociferous . . . bellowing in its sooty throat").

The reverse process, that of identifying living beings with the house, completes the partly humorous impregnation of character and environment each with the other. The very word is used to indicate that the house and Hepzibah are of the same stuff. She had dwelt too much alone," says Hawthorne, "too long in the Pyncheon-house—until her very brain was impregnated with the dry-rot of its timbers" (IV, 55). Her sighs are "like a gust of chill, damp wind out of a long-closed vault" (II, 32). The joints of her knees "creak" (II, 30) just as do the carpetless stairs of the house (V, 65). As with "rusty," "venerable," and "lugubrious," one metaphor links the house and its atmosphere, the hens and Hepzibah: "the strange horror of a turban" (II, 39) on her head, which is comparable to the structure of the mansion, is humorously applied to the degenerated race of fowls: "The distinguishing mark of the hens was a crest, of lamentably scanty growth, in these latter days, but so oddly and wickedly analogous to Hepzibah's turban . . ." (VI, 79). The analogy is further extended at the beginning of chapter XV which, after Phoebe's departure, fittingly recaptures the gloomy atmosphere at the outset of the romance:

> As for Hepzibah, she seemed not merely possessed with the east wind, but to be, in her very person, only another phase of this gray and sullen spell of weather; the East Wind itself, grim and disconsolate, in a rusty black silk-gown, and with a turban of cloud-wreaths on its head! (192)

It is this passage which reminds one most strongly of a paragraph in Poe's Usher tragedy. Like all of Hawthorne's Gothic paraphernalia in the romance, it differs from Poe's lurid vision by its persistent touch of quaintness and by its limited range and power.

Thus far we have observed the author establishing a close metaphorical association between the House of the Seven Gables, Hepzibah, and the hens by employing word patterns of rustiness, lugubriousness, and venerableness. The woof woven back and forth across the fixed threads of the warp in the loom of doom and gloom leaves the other figures out of the weft. Only Venner is tangentially touched through the dignity of his age and the shabbiness of his hat. While in a piece of Gothic fiction proper one atmosphere pervades all, we encounter several "atmospheres" as well as "spheres" in Hawthorne's work. The atmosphere surrounding heroine, habitation, and fowls is indeed a "cold, moist, pitiless" one in which "nothing can flourish" except the moss and the weeds (XV, 192). But even its somberness is alleviated (for the reader, not for the victim) by humor and sympathy. Only once do we find Hepzibah enlivened by the "invigorating breath of a fresh outward atmosphere" (III, 48). This occurs after her forced decision to give up her genteel seclusion for the wholesome if vulgar venture of a cent-shop. Usually she gazes forth "as from another sphere" of "habitual sluggishness" (V, 69). Her sphere is circumscribed by passivity, the past, and castles in the air. Phoebe's domain, on the other hand, is "in the midst of practical affairs" (V, 73), "in the Actual" (IX, 122), and "among common things," as Holgrave remarks toward the end (XX, 259). Light and loveliness surround her existence and activities like a shield. She counteracts, and is in her turn but little and wholesomely influenced by, whatever is old, morbid, dusky, gloomy. "The sordid and ugly luxuriance of gigantic weeds, that grew in the angle of the house, and the heavy projection that overshadowed her, and the time-worn frame-work of the door:—none of these things belonged to her sphere," Hawthorne remarks (IV, 62–63). After all, Phoebe stems from a collateral branch in the Pyncheon family tree. Finally, there is the Judge's "malevolent" sphere (XXI, 270) within whose influence none of the other Pyncheons can exist.

Though the novelist is at pains to differentiate between sister and brother by leaving the latter out of the fateful web and endowing him with the hallmark of a Sybarite and a natural affinity with the beautiful, the outdoors, the sunshine, he nevertheless chains the two together as self-jailed and self-buried. Flight proves illusory. The first attempt on a Sunday morning fails and drives them back into the house.

> They could not flee; their jailer had but left the door ajar, in mockery, and stood behind it, to watch them stealing out. At the threshold, they felt his pitiless gripe upon them. For, what other dungeon is so dark as one's own heart! What jailer so inexorable as one's self! (XI, 147)

Clifford, "this long-buried man," is "summoned forth from his living tomb" (I, 23), but continues to be haunted by "the shadow of a cavern or a dungeon" (VII, 97) and has "the close prison-atmosphere yet lurking in his breath" (XIV, 189). Hepzibah, his fellow prisoner, heaves a "sigh, like a gust of chill, damp wind out of a long-closed vault" on the first morning (II, 32), later aptly descends "into the sepulchral depths of her reminiscences" (IV, 55), mistrusts her "imprisoned joy" and hides it "in the dungeon of her heart" even on the day of Clifford's long-awaited return (VII, 90). Like her brother, she is "an enslaved spirit" (III, 40). Even Alice's harpischord "looked more like a coffin than anything else" (V, 66). When "this pair of strangely enfranchised prisoners" (XVII, 221) makes a renewed attempt to escape from the doomed house where the Judge sits dead in "tomblike seclusion" (XVIII, 242), it is to be expected that the deserted mansion lives on in Clifford's imagination as "a rusty ... old dungeon" (XVII, 224), that he takes a violent stand against man's habit of building durable houses which make him "a prisoner for life in brick, and stone, and old worm-eaten timber" (XVII, 223) and that, when the "owls" alight at a solitary station, they end up in front of a church and a farm house both strongly resembling the Pyncheon home. They are back to where they set out from.

II

All the metaphors discussed so far can be subsumed under what Kenneth Burke would call the dramatic alignment of a work of art. They help to establish the equational structure of *The House of the Seven Gables* and point to what goes with what. They are essentially static, signalling back, not forward.

Three further sets of verbal patterns are somewhat more concerned with the progress of the plot and the solution of problems vexing to the critic. The first of these sheds some light on the interaction of past, present, and future. By way of excusing himself for bothering the reader with the antecedents of the Pyncheon story prior to the narrative time, Hawthorne remarks: "Still, there will be a connection with the long past . . . which, if adequately translated to the reader, would serve to illustrate how much of old material goes to make up the freshest novelty of human life" (I, 10). It is at this point that one would like to marshal old Uncle Venner, neglected by critics, into the limelight. He is an immemorial personage, "the most ancient existence, whether of man or thing, in Pyncheon-street, except the House of the Seven Gables, and perhaps the elm that overshadowed it" (IV, 56). Yet his toughness and vigorousness still "enabled him to fill a place which would else have been vacant, in the apparently crowded world" (IV, 55–56). Venner is a veteran more venerable than rusty, "a miscellaneous old gentleman, partly himself, but, in good measure, somebody else; patched together, too, of different epochs; an epitome of times and fashions" (IV, 57). Even in his Sunday best he is "neatly patched on each elbow" (X, 134). He is, in fact, "the man of patches" (X, 135) and, more importantly, "the patched philosopher" (XIX, 246). These phrases should come to mind in connection with an authorial comment on Holgrave's fretting over the oppressive weight of the past on men's lives. "His error lay," says Hawthorne, "in supposing that this age, more than any past or future one, is destined to see the tattered garments of Antiquity exchanged for a new suit, instead of gradually renewing themselves by patchwork" (XII, 156). Venner's coat is the walking symbol of a feasible compromise between the aristocratic pretensions of Hepzibah's buried life and the daguerreotypist's democratic iconoclasm echoed by Clifford in a fit of lightheaded enthusiasm. This compromise—the realization that the freshest novelty of human life is made up of much old material—is arrived at by Holgrave only at the very end.

The second set of metaphors giving direction to the drift of the romance is that of the stream of life and man's necessary plunge into it. This set—the Wakefieldian theme in much of Hawthorne's fiction—concerns the social dimension of *The House of the Seven Gables*. Phoebe, so healthy in every other respect, would seem to represent the norm. In a beautiful, autobiographically inspired passage the author pays tribute to her character:

> This natural tunefulness made Phoebe seem like a bird in a shadowy tree, or conveyed the idea that the stream of life warbled through her heart, as a brook sometimes warbles through a pleasant little dell. It betokened the cheeriness of an active temperament finding joy in its activity, and therefore rendering it beautiful; it was a New England trait—the stern old stuff of Puritanism, with a gold thread in the web. (V, 69)

Hepzibah is characterized by an inertness and seclusion which tally both with the author's description of the "paltry rivulet of life that flowed through the garden of the Pyncheon-house" (X, 133) and with Holgrave's suggestion that a family should not be "planted" but that "once in every half-century, at longest, a family should be merged into the great, obscure mass of humanity, and forget all about its ancestors" and that "human blood, in order to keep its freshness, should run in hidden streams" (XII, 160). This is precisely what the Maules had done long ago; they had taken "that downright plunge" into obscurity (I, 26), while within the Pyncheon precinct only the bees "plunged into the squash-blossoms" (X, 128). It is Clifford who feels the (for a Pyncheon of his generation, suicidal) urge to plunge into the stream of life. His energy seems surprising, for he "was probably accustomed to a sad monotony of life, not so much flowing in a stream, however sluggish, as stagnating in a pool around his feet" (VII, 98). Nevertheless, when he watches a political procession pass by in the street from the arched window, he instinctively responds to "the rush and roar of the human tide." It so fascinates him "as a mighty river of life, massive in its tide, and black with mystery, and, out of its depths, calling to the kindred depth within him" that he, the born egoist, can hardly be restrained from "plunging into the surging stream of human sympathies" (XI, 143).

What he is here with difficulty prevented from doing and what he shrinks from on the Sabbath morning, he ventures after Judge

Jaffrey's death. Together with his passive sister, he precipitately plunges into what he thinks is life—but the attempt is foredoomed:

> The world's broad, bleak atmosphere was all so comfortless! Such, indeed, is the impression which it makes on every new adventurer, even if he plunge into it while the warmest tide of life is bubbling through his veins. What then must it have been to Hepzibah and Clifford—so time-stricken as they were, yet so like children in their inexperience—as they left the door-step, and passed from beneath the wide shelter of the Pyncheon-elm. (XVII, 217)

Not only does the flight take a circular course—not a "spiral" one, as Clifford imagines—but the pair soon find themselves "adrift" (XVII, 217). Instead of making them actors, participants in life, the train ride reduces them to the passive role of spectators. This scene is Hawthorne's comment on the human predicament. The two Pyncheons and their fellow travellers are hurried along.

> New people continually entered. Old acquaintances . . . continually departed. Here and there, amid the rumble and the tumult, sat one asleep. Sleep; sport; business; graver or lighter study;—and the common and inevitable movement onward! It was life itself! (XVII, 221)

The world, the midst of life, is revealed as a mechanic movement through space. Meanwhile, the dead Judge, too, is "adrift in chaos" (XVIII, 237) and the current of human life makes a small eddy over the depth of his death (XIX, 250).

The last set of metaphors, which appears to be a controlling one, is the idea of life as a theatre. In the early parts of the romance, the metaphor centers on the seriocomically conceived old maiden. She is "a deeply tragic character that contrasted irreconcilably with the ludicrous pettiness of her employment" (II, 36): unsuited for the roles of seamstress and instructress, the "tragedy is enacted" (II, 36) as "our heroine" stoops to become the hucksteress of a cent-shop, with the readers "the spectators of her fate" (II, 37). It is the fate of a patrician lady turned by necessity into a plebeian woman. Before long, one sees her unfit even for this inconspicuous part which she gladly resigns to Phoebe, one of "the real actors in life's stirring scenes" (V, 71).

In chapter XI, "The Arched Window," the dramatic metaphor is developed. The window is transformed into a front seat from which "the life of the street" and "a portion of the great world's movement" may be witnessed (XI, 138). It is shaded by a pair of curtains and opens on to a porch which had formerly been a balcony. Seated there, Clifford watches the Italian boy's performance with his barrel organ presenting "a company of little figures, whose sphere and habitation was in the mahogany case of his organ." This "fortunate little society," which makes "life literally a dance," does "enjoy a harmonious existence in which every individual is employed according to his faculties. But is it really fortunate? Half-reluctantly, the narrator passes a biting judgment on the show:

> Possibly, some cynic, at once merry and bitter, had desired to signify, in this pantomimic scene, that we mortals, whatever our business or amusement . . . all dance to one identical tune, and, in spite of our ridiculous activity, bring nothing finally to pass. For the most remarkable aspect of the affair was, that, at the cessation of the music, everybody was petrified at once, from the most extravagant life into a dead torpor. (XI, 141)

His final suggestion to "reject the whole moral of the show" (XI, 142) only underscores the lesson taught by the "automatic community," as the puppets are called later (XIX, 251).

From this point on, the metaphor becomes still more inclusive and foreshadows as well as explains two later events: the spectacle of the political procession which the onlooker feels to be "fool's play" (XI, 143) and the train ride, another dance to an identical tune where "the merry players fled unconsciously along" (XVII, 220).

The theatrical metaphor has still a different application. Matthew Maule, the carpenter endowed with powers "pretty much like the stage-manager of a theatre" (XIII, 164), commits the sin of converting a human being into an automaton at his beck and bidding. After finishing his story, Holgrave becomes aware of much the same (hypnotic) sway over his listener Phoebe. "She leaned slightly towards him, and seemed almost to regulate her breath by his" (XIV, 182). Out of his saving "quality of reverence for another's individuality" (XIV, 183), he resists the temptation that had made his ancestor guilty. Though renouncing the sorcerer's part, he nevertheless continues, as "a privileged and meet spectator," to study the Pyncheon "drama" which, he speculates, is drawing to its close: " 'I cannot help fancying that Destiny is arranging its fifth act for a catastrophe' " (XIV, 187–188). Phoebe, to whom Holgrave assigns a providential major role in this play, does not like his detached analytical attitude:

> 'You talk as if this old house were a theatre; and you seem to look at Hepzibah's and Clifford's misfortunes, and those of generations before them, as a tragedy, such as I have seen acted in the hall of a country-hotel; only the present one appears to be played exclusively for your amusement! I do not like this. The play costs the performers too much—and the audience is too cold-hearted!" (XIV, 187)

The plot of the romance, an "intermingling of tragedy with mirth" (IX, 253), is unriddled, for Holgrave, by the guilty Judge's preordained expiatory demise, and, for all concerned, by the artist's revelation of his descent and his part as "the old wizard" in this "long drama of wrong and retribution" (XXI, 272).

III

There are more metaphorical patterns to be investigated. The clusters isolated above are among the more conspicuous and consistent ones. Some—such as the running allusions to "iron"—are incidental while others—such as light, dark, gold, cycles—are pervasive and diffuse.

The House of the Seven Gables is beyond doubt "a rich, delightful, imaginative work, larger and more various than its companions, and full of all sorts of deep intentions, of interwoven threads of suggestion," as James thought in 1879. Hawthorne himself had written to Fields that "many passages of the book ought to be finished with the minuteness of a Dutch picture in order to give them their proper effect." Finished in this manner they certainly were, and the foregoing analysis of selected metaphorical chains bears witness to the novelist's precise attention to detail. But the results were not altogether happy, for we have a picture rather than a plot, and figures that are fixed once for all in a *tableau vivant*. And Newton Arvin's complaint that the book suffers from a kind of woodenness in its narrative movement is only too just:

> The scene is set elaborately . . . ; the lines are drawn and the colors disposed with the last subtlety; all the properties are in exquisite keeping, and the lights are adjusted and readjusted with marvelous

atmospheric skill; but the action, in the midst of this impeccable "atmosphere", is halting, torpid, and badly emphasized.

One of the reasons for this woodenness may be seen in the fact that the essential dramatic conflict—the repeated attempts to break away from the house and all that it stands for—is launched too late: the first half of the book, up to chapter XI, is concerned with the arrangement of scene and backdrop and the introduction of the figures, including two "guests." Another reason may lie in the fact that Hawthorne's figures and the metaphors tagged on to them remain static. In Faulkner's Lucas Burch there is a metaphorical course of development: ordinarily mulelike, the rascal becomes in succession snakelike, doglike, wolflike, and ratlike on the day of his flight. Hawthorne's characters in *The House of the Seven Gables* do not progress: Hepzibah remains rusty, Clifford remains torpid, both remain self-jailed and self-buried, Venner remains venerable and so forth. A third reason for the narrative woodenness of the novel may be found in the fact that Hawthorne practically settles the issue before the conflict is enacted. He enmeshes his protagonists in metaphorical nets from which they cannot escape: he links Hepzibah with the house, the house with Hepzibah, the brother with his sister. Both are ghosts to the world and remain so, and the logical line of development leads to the situation reached at the end of chapter XVII and stops there. This situation is an externalization of their fate. At the wayside station, their farthest point from home, they are closer home than they ever were, and they know it.

Which brings us to the much-written-about "prosperous close" of the book. Is this close the proper resolution of a tragedy that had been steering so long toward its due catastrophe? The Judge's timely exit? An avowal of love that makes the earth Eden again? The timely establishment of Clifford's innocence? The opportune news of the decease of the Judge's only son (by cholera!)? The absurd removal of the dramatis personae to the Judge's elegant country seat (if only for the present)? Clifford's partial recovery? Holgrave's astounding about-face? Hepzibah's unscrupulous acceptance of a fortune that has come her way from a dead enemy? And, to crown it all, the indefatigable process of egg-laying suddenly started by the hens? The end is contrived and specious. "The forces of disintegration are represented as in full play," Arvin remarks, "so truly in full play that the happy outcome must be felt to be far too little organic." At the level of metaphor at least,

Hepzibah and Clifford are not so easily liberated and redeemed as Hawthorne and some defenders of the novel's ending would like to have us believe, and the image of life represented by the organ grinder's mechanical people may well have been the intended final truth which the author retracted after it had become too late to do so without affecting the credibility of the story.

William B. Dillingham

Structure and Theme

Most critics of *The House of the Seven Gables* fail to discover any structural pattern. The usual conclusion is that the book consists of a series of episodes tied loosely together by the theme of an inherited curse. Rudolph Von Abele has written that *The House*, in regard to structure, is "loose and atomistic." He objects to the "lyric flights about Clifford's, Hepzibah's and Holgrave's personalities," which "take up fully a third of the book . . . without contributing anything but a kind of irrevelant whimsicality. . . ." For Herbert Gorman, the work "is no more than a series of tales relating to one family. As a novel the book falls to pieces and the reader is confronted with varying ingredients that do not, by any manner of reasoning, form a unified ensemble." Newton Arvin states that "the principle of coherence" among the "scenes" is "less

---

"Structure and Theme in *The House of the Seven Gables*", *Nineteenth Century Fiction,* vol. XIV, No. 1, pp. 59-70 (June 1959). Copyright © 1959 by the Regents of the University of California. Reprinted by permission of the author and the Regents.

dramatic than pictorial." George Woodberry sees *The House* as "a succession of stories bound together" with a "lax unity."

Admittedly, the plot of *The House*, as Austin Warren has said, can be viewed as an "unavoidable nuisance." It is frequently interrupted by long character delineations, flights into the past, musings over matters that are irrelevant to the action of the story. When the various episodes and apparent digressions are considered thematically, however, the work takes on a unity not recognizable when it is viewed solely as a narrative. Despite the superficial motif of an inherited curse, the real theme concerns the necessity of man's participation in what Holgrave terms "the united struggle of mankind." Hawthorne projects his theme in a series of antitheses. Poverty is contrasted with riches, the present with the past, aristocracy with democracy, youth with age, greed with unselfishness, the complex with the simple, appearance with reality, pride with humbleness, the isolated with the unisolated. And each contrast subtly throws light on the theme. For example, the character delineations of Clifford and Phoebe, ridiculed by the critics, show an isolated character contrasted with an unisolated character and deftly point up the pathos and hopelessness of a state of psychological isolation. Again, the scene in chapter xviii that pictures the dead Judge alone in the House of the Seven Gables offers a contrast between the real and the apparent, between the real Judge Pyncheon and the Judge as the deceived people of his town see him. It is a dramatic representation of the hypocrisy that results from Judge Pyncheon's psychological isolation from the "united struggle of mankind."

Thus the "varying ingredients," although not all contributing to the plot, do contribute to the theme, the most important unifying element. Of the various contrasts that pervade the entire novel, three are especially dominant in three different parts, and to these principal contrasts the novel owes its major theme. The first six chapters stress the desirability of a democratic way of life over an aristocratic one. With the introduction of Clifford in chapter vii the theme of psychological isolation comes into the foreground and is emphasized through chapter xiv, mainly in contrasts of Clifford, Hepzibah, and the Judge with unisolated characters. The last seven chapters constantly reflect the main theme by pointing up the dichotomy between appearance and reality. To illustrate the structural pattern and theme a rather detailed consideration of each of the three parts is necessary.

I

In chapter i the conflict between the aristocratic Colonel Pyncheon and the plebeian Matthew Maule sets the stage for the strong antithesis of aristocracy and democracy that remains in the foreground for six chapters. When the ancient House of the Seven Gables is first erected by Colonel Pyncheon, he has an openhouse celebration to which he invites both the aristocratic and the plebeian classes. But each class receives different treatment. Two servants observe the guests as they arrive, "pointing some of the guests of the neighborhood of the kitchen, and ushering others into the statelier rooms,—hospitable alike to all, but still with a scrutinizing regard to the high or low degree of each" (p. 25). Thus early in the history of the house a pride in high social degree becomes a part of the Pyncheon tradition, which, like all aristocratic traditions, is based on a flimsy foundation. The symbol of the Pyncheons' absurd claim to superiority is the missing deed to the territory in Maine.

> This impalpable claim, therefore, resulted in nothing more solid than to cherish, from generation to generation, an absurd delusion of family importance, which all along characterized the Pyncheons. It caused the poorest member of the race to feel as if he inherited a kind of nobility, and might yet come into possession of princely wealth to support it [p. 33].

The decline of the Pyncheon aristocracy is indicated in terms of Hepzibah's having to open a cent-shop in order to earn a livelihood. Hawthorne pictures the old maid sympathetically, but, by placing her in opposition to the life around her, also reveals her emptiness and the necessity for her coming out of her proud shell of tradition and becoming a part of the populace. She is

> the final throe of what called itself old gentility. A lady—who had fed herself from childhood with the shadowy food of aristocratic reminiscences, and whose religion it was that a lady's hand soils itself irremediably by doing aught for bread . . . [p. 55].

She must at last step down from her proud and isolated pedestal of aristocracy. And it is her "great life-trial," for this "poorest member of the race" feels as if she "inherited a kind of nobility."

Democracy's triumph over aristocracy is again emphasized in chapter iii with the introduction of a strong representative of democracy, Holgrave, the descendant of Matthew Maule. Speaking to Holgrave of her "gentility," Hepzibah says: "But I was born a lady, and have always lived one; no matter in what narrowness of means, always a lady!" (p. 63). But Holgrave sees through the superficiality of these faded and meaningless titles of "lady" and "gentleman." Rather than conferring any special privileges, they restrict the holder of the titles to an artificial code of behavior that renders him useless to himself and to society. To Hepzibah's statement, Holgrave answers:

"But I was not born a gentleman; neither have I lived like one . . . so . . . you will hardly expect me to sympathize with sensibilities of this kind; though . . . I have some imperfect comprehension of them. These names of gentleman and lady had a meaning, in the past history of the world, and conferred privileges, desirable or otherwise, on those entitled to bear them. In the present—and still more in the future condition of society—they imply, not privilege, but restriction!" [pp. 63–64].

Holgrave speaks further for social equality in answering Hepzibah's complaint that, since she is a "lady," she cannot become involved in the operation of a common cent-shop:

"Hitherto, the life-blood has been gradually chilling in your veins as you sat aloof, within your circle of gentility, while the rest of the world was fighting out its battle with one kind of necessity or another. Henceforth, you will at least have the sense of healthy and natural effort for a purpose, and of lending your strength— be it great or small—to the united struggle of mankind" [63].

In chapter iv Phoebe comes to live in Hepzibah's ancient house and to work in the cent-shop. A Pyncheon in name only, she serves as a foil to her traditional surroundings: "The young girl, so fresh, so unconventional, and yet so orderly and obedient to common rules . . . was widely in contrast . . . with everything about her" (p. 90). In chapter v, "May and November," the antithesis of aristocracy and democracy is most explicit in Hepzibah's lament that Phoebe is an excellent shopkeeper, but not a "lady." But "it would be preferable," writes Hawthorne, "to regard Phoebe as the example of feminine grace and availability combined, in a state of society, if there were any such, where ladies did not exist" (p. 104). In direct contrast with Phoebe, Hawthorne pictures Hepzibah, who is a lady but less desirable in every way:

> To find the born and educated lady, on the other hand, we need look no farther than Hepzibah, our forlorn old maid, in her rustling and rusty silks, with her deeply cherished and ridiculous consciousness of long descent. . . . It was a fair parallel between new Plebeianism and old Gentility [p. 104].

Chapter vi brings together two members of the new democracy, Phoebe and Holgrave, in the traditionally aristocratic Pyncheon garden with its "grass, and foliage, and aristocratic flowers." The deteriorating effect of the social snobbery implicit in an aristocratic way of life is symbolized by the diminutive Pyncheon hens. Like the Pyncheons, the isolated chickens "had degenerated . . . in consequence of too strict a watchfulness" to keep them aloof and pure (p. 113).

An aristocracy emphasizes the excellence and privileges of a few and leads to a dangerous and unwise withdrawal from the world's "united struggle." Thus the express superiority of a state of social equality represents the main theme of the first six chapters. The center of Part I is Hepzibah, the major symbol of a fallen aristocracy. Within this part, Hawthorne arranges each scene so that there are never more than two characters together—usually one plebeian and one aristocrat.

II

Man's need to participate in the world's "united struggle" becomes more apparent in Part II (chapters vii–xiv) as the isolated characters, Clifford, Hepzibah, and the Judge, are studied in contrast to those who are a part of the human brotherhood. Hepzibah, Clifford, and Judge Pyncheon represent three distinct ways in which man is isolated from his fellows. Hepzibah is isolated through pride in tradition and an aristocratic way of life; Clifford through his extreme love of only the beautiful; and Judge Pyncheon through greed. All three have only a partial view of reality. They cannot see life as it is because they are blinded by their characteristic weaknesses of pride, extreme aesthetic sensibility, and greed.

As Hepzibah is the chief figure of a degraded aristocracy in Part I, Clifford, beginning with his introduction in chapter vii, is the man figure of isolation in Part II. Like Hepzibah (but for a different reason), Clifford has always been outside the realm of reality. He had "nothing to do with sorrow; nothing with strife; nothing with the martyrdom which . . . awaits those who have the heart, and will, and conscience, to fight a battle with the world" (p. 134). Clifford's nature isolates him, for "it seemed Clifford's nature to be a Sybarite" (p. 135). He can have no part in the "united struggle of mankind" for he can accept only the beautiful. He cannot feel even the closeness of kinship and love for Hepzibah that she feels for him, for she does not possess the beauty his nature requires for adoration. "How could he—so yellow as she was, so wrinkled, so sad of mien, with that odd uncouthness of a turban on her head, and that most perverse of scowls contorting her brow,—how could he love to gaze at her?" p. 135). But "did he owe her no affection for so much as she had silently given? He owed her nothing. A nature like Clifford's can contract no debts of that kind" (pp. 135–136). Rather than a detriment to his well-being, therefore, the long imprisonment may have been the instrument that saved what little affection Clifford is capable of feeling. For, if

> Clifford . . . had enjoyed the means of cultivating his taste to its utmost perfectibility, that subtle attribute might, before his period, have completely eaten out or filed away his affections. Shall we venture to pronounce, therefore, that his long and black calamity may not have had a redeeming drop of mercy at the bottom? [p. 140].

The third major character, Judge Pyncheon, enters the novel in chapter viii. He represents in his generation a long line of avaricious Pyncheons. Like his ancestors, he is afflicted by "the moral diseases which lead to crime" and "are handed down from one generation to another, by a far surer process of transmission than human law has been able to establish in respect to the riches and honors which it seeks to entail upon posterity" (p. 147). To the world Judge Pyncheon seems kindly and philanthropic. Actually, however, he is separated from mankind. In chapter viii he attempts to bestow his affection upon Phoebe in the cent-shop. He offers to kiss her as a symbol of "acknowledged kindred," but Phoebe, "without design, or only with such instinctive design as gives no account of itself to the intellect," draws away and refuses the kiss (p. 145). Despite the ties of blood between them, she realizes that he is a stranger to her world.

In the first part of chapter viii, the comparison of Judge Pyncheon with his ancestor, the Colonel, indicates the reason for the isolation of both these characters: greed. For, "tradition affirmed that the Puritan had been greedy of wealth; the Judge, too, with all the show of liberal expenditure, was said to be as closefisted as if his grip were of iron" (p. 150). Not only is he selfish with what he already has, but he is ruthless in obtaining more, as is indicated in his first attempted interview with Clifford. This incident establishes the Judge as the villain and reveals the growing conflict between him and his poorer relations, which is the central action of the plot. His "hot fellness of purpose, which annihilated everything but itself," isolates him from mankind (p. 159). He has upset the necessary equilibrium in life by allowing the head to overcome the dictates of the heart. Like Roger Chillingworth, Ethan Brand, and Rappaccini, Judge Pyncheon follows one major ambition to his doom.

In chapter ix the complex and melancholy Clifford again assumes the central position in the theme of isolation as he is contrasted with the bright little Phoebe. As a consequence of Clifford's partial acceptance of reality, "the world never wanted him." Phoebe's nature, on the other hand,

> was not one of those . . . which are most attracted by what is strange and exceptional in human character. The path which would best have suited her was the well-worn track of ordinary life; the companions in whom she would most have delighted were such as one encounters at every turn [p. 173].

Possessing a freshness derived from her kinship with humanity, she is the "only representative of womanhood" who is at least partly able to bring Clifford "back into the breathing world" (p. 170). For, Hawthorne explains, "Persons who have wandered, or been expelled, out of the common track of things . . . desire nothing so much as to be led back. They shiver in their loneliness, be it on a mountain-top or in a dungeon" (p. 170).

The pathos involved in Clifford's isolation is evident as he gazes from behind the arched window upon as much of "the great world's movement" as possible. Hawthorne describes the

> pale, gray, childish, aged, melancholy, yet often simply cheerful, and sometimes delicately intelligent aspect of Clifford, peering from behind the faded crimson of the curtain,—watching the monotony of every-day occurrences with a kind of inconsequential interest and earnestness, and, at every petty throb of his sensibility, turning for sympathy to the eyes of the bright young girl! [pp. 192–193].

In the middle chapter of *The House* (chapter xi) the theme of isolation reaches its peak of intensity in Clifford's actions. As he and Phoebe watch the parade march with all its pomp past the House of the Seven Gables, he realizes his state of isolation from the "one broad mass of existence,—one great life,—one collected body of mankind" (p. 199), and he cannot resist an actual physical attempt to plunge down into the "surging stream of human sympathy."

> He shuddered; he grew pale. . . . At last, with tremulous limbs, he started up, set his foot on the window-sill, and in an instant more would have been in the unguarded balcony. . . . [He was] a wild, haggard figure, his gray locks floating in the wind that waved their banners; a lonely being, estranged from his race . . . [p. 200].

Then Hawthorne clearly describes Clifford's great need to become reunited with the world and hints that this reunion can be accomplished only by death.

> He needed a shock; or perhaps he required to take a deep, deep plunge into the ocean of human life, and to sink down and be covered by its profoundness, and then to emerge, sobered, invigorated, restored to the world and to himself. Perhaps, again, he required nothing less than the great final remedy—death [p. 201].

In the latter part of chapter xi a second attempt "to renew the broken links of brotherhood" involves Hepzibah, who, like Clifford, is cognizant of her aloofness from mankind. Indeed, she

> yearned to take him by the hand, and go and kneel down, they two together,—both so long separate from the world, and, as she now recognized, scarcely friends with Him above,—to kneel down among the people, and be reconciled to God and man at once [p. 203].

But as the two pathetic figures attempt to follow Phoebe to church, they realize that they have lived too long in solitude and that there is no returning. "We have no right among human beings," Clifford says, "no right anywhere but in this old house . . ." (p. 204). As they retreat to the dismal mansion, there is a contrast between the free air of the outside world and the heavy atmosphere of their "jail," the house.

The last three chapters of Part II are concerned mainly with Holgrave, with the story he reads to Phoebe, and with Phoebe's departure. In spite of the immaturity of Holgrave's notions about reform, he does possess some wisdom in matters relating to the isolating effect of the past on the present. "It [the past] lies upon the Present like a giant's dead body!" he tells Phoebe.

> "In fact, the case is just as if a young giant were compelled to waste all his strength in carrying about the corpse of the old giant, his grandfather, who died a long while ago, and only needs to be decently buried. Just think a moment, and it will startle you to see what slaves we are to bygone times . . ." [p. 219].

The story which Holgrave reads to Phoebe emphasizes the two traits which have brought about Maule's Curse and isolated the Pyncheons: greed and pride. Gervayse Pyncheon upset the balance of head and heart and sacrificed his daughter for the promise of wealth. Gervayse's fate is similar to that of Colonel Pyncheon and, much later, to that of Judge Pyncheon.

Except for the judge, all of the main characters are brought together in chapter xiv as Phoebe leaves the old mansion. The contrast between the hopelessly isolated Clifford and Phoebe as she says good-by to him is striking. Her departure takes him even further into the world of solitude. His parting remark to her is: "Go, now!—I feel lonelier than I did" (p. 263). Phoebe's departure terminates the second structural part of the novel. Holgrave sets the scene for the climax, which comes at the beginning of Part III, when he says to Phoebe before she leaves: "I cannot help fancying that Destiny is arranging its fifth act for a catastrophe" (p. 260). From Judge Pyncheon's attempted interview with Clifford in chapter viii to Holgrave's portentous remarks at the end of Part II, there is a general movement of the plot, a building up of the major conflict between Hepzibah, Clifford, and the Judge, toward the climactic scene, which occurs in chapter xv and ends in the Judge's death. The theme of isolation is thus predominant in Part II, and is stressed by the study of the isolated in contrast to the unisolated. As the narrative progresses, it becomes increasingly evident that the isolated figures cannot become reconciled with the world.

III

From the time when Hepzibah's scowl is contrasted with the Judge's smile in chapter xv to the end of the novel, where the events of the story ostensibly terminate in complete felicity, things are clearly not as they seem. Judge Pyncheon, who casts his shadow over this last part of the novel, is portrayed on two levels: as he appears and as he really is. The very title of chapter xv ("The Scowl and the Smile") hints at Hawthorne's concern with the deceptiveness of outward appearance as typified in Hepzibah and the Judge. The townspeople think Hepzibah's scowl reflects her inward nature. Although she is, in reality, warm and kind, her myopic frown stamps her as sour and bitter. In contrast, the Judge seems benevolent but is really a villain of the first order. To the world, he is

> a man of eminent respectability. The church acknowledged it; the state acknowledged it. It was denied by nobody. In all the very extensive sphere of those who knew him . . . there was not an individual—except Hepzibah, and . . . the daguerreotypist . . . who would have dreamed of seriously disputing his claim to a high and honorable place in the world's regard [p. 272].

He is like a marvelously well-built palace with a "deadly hole under the pavement" that contains, unseen from the outside, some secret decay. For, "beneath the show of a marble palace . . . is this man's miserable soul!" (p. 274).

The growing conflict between the avaricious Judge and his relatives in the House of the Seven Gables reaches a climax in chapter xvi, when the Judge demands to see Clifford. In his twisted mind he is sure that Clifford knows the location of a long-lost Pyncheon treasure. The climax of the novel is thus brought about by the Judge's reliance on false judgment made from appearance. For, the only gold Clifford has "at his command" is "but shadowy gold," and is "not the stuff to satisfy Judge Pyncheon!" (pp. 288–289). Appearance then leads to another misunderstanding. Hepzibah finds the Judge dead, and Clifford urges her to flee with him from the house. Everything points to the conclusion that Clifford has murdered the Judge and thus ended the constant threat to his well-being.

In chapter xviii, Hawthorne offers a clue to the chief theme in the section by the title of the chapter, "Governor Pyncheon." The labels "Governor," "Colonel," and "Judge" represent titles which to the world signify integrity and honor, but which, in the case of the Judge and his ancestors, denote, in truth, a marked dishonesty. Hawthorne pictures the dead Judge sitting alone in the House of the Seven Gables while a storm rages outside; and by describing all his scheduled activities for the day in which he dies, reveals the dichotomy between appearance and reality in the Judge's life.

The last three chapters compose the denouement of the novel, and there is much explication of plot details in these chapters. The Judge's death is a natural one of the same type that overcame the Colonel, not murder as it has seemed to be. The daguerreotypist is shown in his true identity as a descendant of Matthew Maule. Many other details, such as the location of the missing document, are explained and the story comes to a close with no questions unanswered.

In these final chapters a constant undertone reminds us of the contrast between appearance and reality, both in plot details and in Judge Pyncheon's life. The morning after the Judge's death, when the summer storm has subsided, even the ancient House of the Seven Gables appears to be a place with a pleasant history (chapter xix). "So little faith is due to external appearance, that there was really an inviting aspect over the venerable edifice, conveying an idea that its history must be a decorous and happy one . . ." (p. 337). This undertone is exemplified down through the last chapter of the book in remarks concerning Judge Pyncheon. In chapter xxi, Hawthorne writes: "Thus Jaffrey Pyncheon's inward criminality . . . was, indeed, black and damnable; while its mere outward show and positive commission was the smallest that could possibly consist with so great a sin" (p. 370).

Thematically the most important, and indeed the most striking, example of this ironic undertone comes in the ending. Hepzibah, Clifford, Holgrave, and Phoebe leave the ancient house to live in the Judge's country home with the intention of having the "patched philosopher," Uncle Venner, join them later. These actions seem to indicate that happiness has at last been achieved by Hepzibah and Clifford, who have inherited the Judge's fortune and are rid of his threat. But the level of the apparent here, as in other places in Part III, is not to be mistaken for the real. A recent criticism maintains that

> the Maule-Pyncheons ride happily away from the House of the Seven Gables to possess the future in a merger of bright fortunes —almost a fairy story ending for Clifford and Hepzibah. . . . It's about as pessimistic as Cinderella. . . . Old Maid Pyncheon closes up her cent shop 'and rides off in her carriage with a couple of hundred thousand. . . .'

And this is precisely what happens. But to assume that the fortune which Hepzibah and Clifford inherit will mean perfect bliss for them is a failure to understand the fundamental traits of these characters and the main theme of the novel. Hepzibah had been fortunate indeed when she was forced to open a cent-shop, step down from her isolated pedestal of "imaginary rank," and become a part of the "surging stream of human sympathy." The epoch of Hepzibah's contact with the human struggle is short-lived, however. With her inheritance of the Judge's fortune she can step back upon her pedestal of gentility, there to remain isolated and lost.

Clifford, we should remember, is a Sybarite. With the loss of Phoebe, "his only representative of womanhood," to Holgrave, Clifford has passed his greatest happiness. He now has "the means of cultivating his taste to its utmost perfectibility." In the closing pages Hawthorne writes that Clifford has "all the appliances now at command to gratify his instinct for the Beautiful . . ." (p. 372). And the result can only be isolation and an "eating out of his affections." For the three chief characters of the novel, the ending is anything but happy, in spite of appearances. The Judge dies isolated from man and God because of his greed. Hepzibah will again be a "lady," isolated from the "united struggle," and Clifford will no longer be forced to see life as it is; he can now view only the beautiful. Ironically, therefore, Holgrave's remark in chapter xiv that "Destiny is arranging its fifth act for a catastrophe" applies not to the death of Judge Pyncheon, which certainly is no catastrophe, but to the tragedy that is to befall Hepzibah and Clifford upon their inheritance of the Judge's fortune. It is an echo of the statement Hawthorne recorded in his notebooks: "To inherit a great fortune. To inherit a great misfortune."

Structurally, then, *The House* is composed of a series of antitheses with three particular contrasts dominating the book. To these dominant contrasts the work owes its major theme: the necessity of man's close communion with his fellow beings. Primarily because of its basic weakness in plot, *The House* is not Hawthorne's best work. It is, nevertheless, much more than a series of unrelated tales that contribute nothing to the total effect but a kind of "irrelevant whimsicality." Organized under a pervading theme, the seemingly diverse elements of the novel can be said to form a "unified ensemble."

Francis Joseph Battaglia

New Light on Old Problems

Many twentieth-century commentators on Hawthorne's *The House of the Seven Gables*—probably the majority of them—have found it necessary to note serious failings in the work. The censures are in a sense as different as the men who registered them, but I think they can be fairly summarized as: (1) objection to the plot as lacking coherent action and to the narrative method as partial cause of this difficulty; (2) objection to the conclusion as being artificial or forced; and (3) objection to the short-sightedness of the author in saying in his Preface and as comment within the story something which the story itself confutes. Structure, conclusion, and theme have all proved problematical.

These charges are quite considerable in range and weight, and the study which resulted in this paper was originally concerned with only the second of them. The evidence, however, which has suggested to me that the ending of Hawthorne's novel is neither artificial nor forced, in turn suggests that the plot of the novel has

---

Reprinted by permission of the Modern Language Association from "*The House of the Seven Gables*: New Lights on Old Problems," *PMLA,* vol. 82, pp. 579-590 (December 1967).

been in a very important particular generally misread. The whole structure of the novel is thus implicated in a discussion of its ending. In addition, an explanation of the conclusion of a novel can hardly be valid if it cannot account for the narrator's own statements. Hawthorne has told us both in the Preface and in the novel proper what *The House of the Seven Gables* is about; his statements have to be dealt with. I wish to suggest that the conclusion of Hawthorne's novel is fitting; doing so will entail consideration of the first and third objections as well. The task would be even larger were not objections one and two different sides of the same coin.

Austin Warren wrote of *The House of the Seven Gables* in 1948: "[Hawthorne's] method is almost that of a succession of tableaux. The characters do not really develop or change. . . . Nor does he show us the characters acting on each other. . . . Scenes of conversation . . . are expository, and do not advance the action." F. O. Matthiessen and Newton Arvin are probably the most notable among the Hawthorne scholars who hold similar views of the plot of *The House of the Seven Gables*. The action of the novel has generally been found episodic rather than cumulative; characterization seems to compound the difficulty, for the persons of the novel neither develop nor interact; Hawthorne's narrative penchant is responsible for the *stasis* of his characters, for he would rather describe them than have them reveal themselves in action: even in dialogue they do not affect each other. The general objection to the novel's plot includes an ancillary concern for character development and the use of dialogue.

Hawthorne's ending to the novel has likewise, to quote Matthiessen, "satisfied very few. Although Phoebe's marriage with Holgrave . . . is meant finally to transcend the old brutal separation of classes . . . the reconciliation is somewhat too lightly made." Phoebe and Holgrave emerge as lovers in the closing chapters and allow Hawthorne to arrange a happy finish to his book. But this resolution seems contrived; the final chapters are too late a point for a character to *begin* to undergo his basic change. Arvin has called Holgrave's love for Phoebe "factitious dramatically."

These objections could be further documented with quotations from the work of Henry James, George Woodberry, Herbert Gorman, Mark Van Doren, and other more recent writers, but I hope to have established at least that they are customary charges against Hawthorne's work. Insofar as there is one, they represent a consensus of opinion about the plot and conclusion of *The House of the Seven Gables.* They are not discrete points, of course. Both objections deal with a different facet of the same novel; the first overlaps the second; and characterization figures prominently in each. Even more than is intimated in this statement of their similarity, however, the charges have a common basis.

The novel has been found slow-moving, and lacking a "strong narrative line"; very little seems to happen. Rudolph Van Abele considers a third of the book ("between the seventh and fifteenth chapters") to be "irrelevant." On the other hand, the denouement is said to unravel much too fast, with insufficient preparation for the changes which take place there. These difficulties admit the possibility of common solution: if the characters of the novel did gradually change and develop, but for some reason their alterations had not been recognized, students of the novel would understandably have remarked both that its plot was weak and that its denouement was abrupt. If the novel depends for its narrative line on progressive shifts in the attitudes of its characters, and these shifts are not discerned, the reader is very apt to find the work more like tableaux than genuine narrative. W. B. Dillingham began his article on "Structure and Theme in *The House of the Seven Gables*" disagreeing with those who see no structural pattern in the work, but in closing he conceded a "basic weakness in plot."

Although it entails the suggestion—which anyone aware of the extent and value of existing Hawthorne scholarship would not make lightly—that most writers of *The House of the Seven Gables* have failed to discern an essential feature of the novel, I will maintain here that the solution just broached in hypothetical form is the accurate one, i.e., the novel has been in a very important particular generally misread. A modified reading of the middle events of the novel comprises my main reason for thinking the conclusion appropriate (I); it also provides cause for a revision of critical opinion on the novel's narrative structure (II). The question of theme and the author's statements about it will be taken up after these matters (III).

I

"The conclusion is unspeakably awkward. For thematic reasons Hawthorne was absolutely forced to marry Phoebe and Holgrave —but with so little interest in the business that he could not bother to prepare for the event by showing them developing so much as a real interest in each other." Thus Philip Young restated the customary objection to the ending of *The House of the Seven Gables* in 1957. The appraisal is, however, unfair to the novel, because Hawthorne's preparations for the final union of Holgrave and Phoebe have been quite elaborate. Love between them is explicitly suggested as early as Chapter xii; their romance is fully under way in Chapter xiv, and Hawthorne in the same chapter is at pains to see that the reader is aware of it.

Chapter xii, "The Daguerreotypist," recounts a conversation between Phoebe and Holgrave in the Pyncheon Garden. In light of the fact that Hawthorne's conversations have been said not to advance the plot and they characterize individuals rather than show them interacting, it is notable that the author specifies this conversation as unique instead of typical. Having devoted several pages to a general account of the daguerreotypist and his views, the narrator says: "But our business is with Holgrave, as we find him on this particular afternoon, and in the arbor of the Pyncheon garden." Hawthorne goes on to distinguish further the conversation from others that have occurred, and he is already beginning to mark the signs of romantic feeling in Holgrave. A few pages earlier the author had noted that Phoebe "scarcely thought him affectionate in his nature. He was too calm and cool an observer. . . . He seemed to be in quest of mental food; not heart-sustenance" (pp. 177-178). On this particular afternoon, however, Holgrave's demeanor could not be so described: "Her thought had scarcely done him justice, when it pronounced him cold; or if so, he had grown warmer, now" (pp. 181–182). Having called Holgrave "warmer," Hawthorne uses other terms suggestive of romantic affection in preparing us for the conversation which will continue for two chapters: "the artist . . . was beguiled, by some silent charm of hers, to talk freely of what he dreamed of doing in the world. He poured himself out as to another self" (p. 182). Holgrave's customary detachment might lead us to think that his interest in Phoebe was "Platonic" rather than romantic, but Hawthorne playfully suggests it would not have struck an observer that way: "Very possibly, he forgot Phoebe while he talked to her, and was moved only by the inevitable tendency of thought, when rendered sympathetic by enthusiasm and emotion, to flow into the first safe reservoir which it finds. But, had you peeped at them through the chinks of the garden fence, the young man's earnestness and heightened color might have led you to suppose that he was making love to the young girl!" (p. 182). "Love" is alluded to, I think for the first time in connection with the pair.

All of this, though revealing, is but preparation, for Holgrave and Phoebe do not emerge definitely as lovers until Chapter xiv. Hawthorne, however, has at this point already rather clearly admitted romantic love to his plot.

To be ready for Chapter xiv, we need note one further thing about the conversation at its outset. Not answering Phoebe's query as to why he chose to live in the old Pyncheon house, Holgrave begins his famous radical discourse against things antique. "Shall we never, never get rid of this Past?" he cries. "It lies upon the Present like a giant's dead body!" (p. 182). Expounding on his theme, he proposes that each generation should build its own houses; public buildings should be constructed of such materials that they would crumble to ruin once in twenty years to remind men of the need for reform in the institutions they represent. At this point he returns to the subject of the House of Seven Gables, and recommends its fiery purgation: "Now this old Pyncheon-house! Is it a wholesome place to live in, with its black shingles, and the green moss that shows how damp they are?—its dark, low-studded rooms?—its grime and sordidness, which are the crystallization on its walls of the human breath, that has been drawn and exhaled here, in discontent and anguish? The house ought to be purified with fire—purified till only its ashes remain!" (p. 184). The House of Seven Gables will again be Holgrave's topic in Chapter xiv.

The daguerreotypist has written a story detailing alleged events of Pyncheon family history. With a little encouragement from Phoebe, he is soon reading it aloud. In the tale Alice Pyncheon falls prey to the hypnotic arts of Matthew Maule, and recounting the incident, complete with gestures, Holgrave inadvertently brings Phoebe to the verge of a trance which would give him power over her similar to that gained over young Alice by the mesmerist of his story. Maurice Beebe has aptly observed that Holgrave's refusal to exercise hypnotic power over Phoebe is an important step in his regeneration: "He ceases to be the detached observer and becomes a participator, not merely 'using' life but living it." Immediately after he takes this step, his love and Phoebe's kindle.

Chapter xiv, "Phoebe's Good-By," begins with Holgrave's refusal to complete Phoebe's spell; instead he joshes her back to her normal state, chiding her for falling asleep at his dull story. Seemingly abruptly, and quite atypically, Hawthorne turns to a description of the sun going down and the moon rising. Even more uncommonly, he has an apparently nonhuman, non-moral, non-spiritual force intervene directly in his story. Moonbeams, "chang[ing] the character of the lingering daylight," "transfigured" what they fell on "by a charm of romance." "They softened and embellished the aspect of the old house." The "reviving influence" also fell on the artist and "made him feel—what he sometimes almost forgot, thrust so early, as he had been, into the rude struggle of man with man—how youthful he still was" (p. 213).

In this unusual passage Hawthorne seems to be invoking moon-power, or the power of a moon-goddess, as an operative force in his story. The moon has some of the faculties of Artemis, the benign Hellenic and pre-Hellenic deity who had particular care for youth and growth, the paradoxical Woman-goddess of childbirth and chastity whom the moon represented. Even if this connection is pertinent, however, what does, or at least should, an Artemis-moon have to do with *The House of the Seven Gables?* Mythological machinery seems out of character for Hawthorne.

The agent at work is probably not mythological, though the connection with Artemis seems worth making because one of the other names of the goddess was "Phoebe." Without suggesting any relevance for Chapter xiv, Hyatt Waggoner thought the Phoebe-Artemis congruence significant enough to devote half a paragraph to it in his introduction to a recent edition of *The House of the Seven Gables*. It is an engaging possibility that the "reviving influence" of moonlight on Holgrave stands for the influence of Phoebe; but this gloss is ultimately unsatisfactory, for Phoebe herself changes under the moon's beams:

> "I am sensible of a great charm in this brightening moonlight. . . . I never cared much about moonlight before. What is there, I wonder, so beautiful in it, tonight?"
> "And you have never felt it before?" inquired the artist . . .
> "Never," answered Phoebe; "and life does not look the same, now that I have felt it so." (p. 214)

Rather than Phoebe's power, the moon-scene is, I think, Hawthorne's allegorical rendering of the coming of love to the pair. Holgrave, who has been made to feel "how youthful he still was," offers Phoebe this very explanation, though he hardly realizes yet what his words mean:

> "Sometimes—always, I suspect, unless one is exceedingly unfortunate—there comes a sense of second youth, gushing out of the heart's *joy at being in love*; or, possibly, it may come to crown some other grand festival in life, if any other such there be" [italics mine] . . .
> "I hardly think I understand you," said Phoebe.
> "No wonder," replied Holgrave, smiling; "for I have told you a secret which I hardly began to know, before I found myself giving it utterance. Remember it, however; and when the truth becomes clear to you, then think of this moonlight scene!" (p. 215)

When the truth does become clear to her—as we shall see—she blushes.

Holgrave's first reaction to love's moonlit influence—which he feels immediately after willing not to take advantage of Phoebe—indicates the extent of the change love will have on him. F. O. Matthiessen has found Hawthorne's handling of the artist later in Chapter xx, "devastating in its limitations. . . . Society no longer looks hostile. When Phoebe is afraid that he will lead her out of her own quiet path, he already knows that the influence is likely to be all the other way." The whole development comes too abruptly, and it is hardly credible that Holgrave would know already at the point of falling in love what effects it will have on him. Chapter xxi bears out his fore-reckoning that love will mollify his social views, for there he voices the wish that Judge Pyncheon had built in stone instead of in wood. The artist, however, falls in love not in the next to last (twentieth) chapter of the book, but in the fourteenth. Moreover, Chapter xiv shows strikingly that Holgrave's radical views are even then being altered. When he "already knows" in Chapter xx that Phoebe will change him more than he will her, Holgrave is exercising hindsight, not precognition.

In Chapter xii, where love was just starting to stir in him, the artist inveighed against the Past and thought incineration the best cure for the ills of the House of Seven Gables. In Chapter xiv after he refuses to gain power over Phoebe's soul, their love burgeons, and the resultant alteration in his perspective is remarkable:

> "After all, what a good world we live in! How good, and beautiful! How young it is, too, with nothing really rotten or age-worn in it! This old house, for example, which sometimes has positively oppressed my breath with its smell of decaying timber! And this garden, where the black mould always clings to my spade, as if I

were a sexton, delving in a graveyard! Could I keep the feeling that now possesses me, the garden would every day be virgin soil, with the earth's first freshness in the flavor of its beans and squashes; and the house!—it would be like a bower in Eden blossoming with the earliest roses that God ever made." (p. 214)

Rather than wishing to burn the Pyncheon house, Holgrave is now possessed by a feeling which makes the garden an Eden of "first freshness" and the House of Seven Gables a bower there. Holgrave's language will be echoed in Hawthorne's description of the couple in Chapter xx, "The Flower of Eden," after they have declared their love: "The bliss, which makes all things true, beautiful, and holy, shone around this youth and maiden. They were conscious of nothing sad or old. They transfigured the earth, and made it Eden again, and themselves the two first dwellers in it" (p. 307). The loving couple will "transfigure" the earth; moonbeams had "transfigured" all in the garden. By Chapter xiv love has already mellowed Holgrave's radical humanitarianism of Chapter xii. This "early" change in the daguerreotypist's social views has to my knowledge received attention from only three twentieth-century writers on Hawthorne. It is important that the change be heeded, however, for otherwise Holgrave's later preference for stone houses, like his love for Phoebe, will seem contrived.

Hawthorne's love story takes one further turn in "Phoebe's Good-By." Chapter xiv brought Holgrave to the test of whether he would be a second Maule to cast a spell over a Pyncheon daughter. He refused, and felt with Phoebe the moonlight power of love. The artist had an inkling of what influence was affecting them, though he hardly anticipated his own words in telling it to Phoebe. She was not sure she understood. Later in the chapter, Hawthorne narrates for us the scene of her realization, and he uses the same technique employed in Chapter vi.

In that chapter Hawthorne describes Phoebe's entering the house to find Hepzibah acting strangely. Clifford has returned, though Phoebe does not know it, and Hawthorne does not tell his readers either until the next chapter. Instead he recounts the scene in such a way as to make the reader aware that information is being withheld from him—Phoebe, for example, hears the footsteps of a person walking with Hepzibah, but does not know who it is. Puzzling over the problem that the author has posed him, the reader may piece together previous hints and foreshadowings to realize that Clifford has come home. But whether the reader realizes or not, Hawthorne has brought heightened attention to the fact that something new has developed in the story.

The same technique draws heightened awareness in Chapter xiv. Two days later after the garden scene with Holgrave in which she felt, but did not understand, the influence of love, Phoebe is taking leave of Clifford and Hepzibah when Clifford cries for her to come "Close!—closer!—and look me in the face!" (p. 220). Under his gaze she realizes what Holgrave's self-discovering explanation had tried to tell her:

> Phoebe soon felt that, if not the profound insight of a seer, yet a more than feminine delicacy of appreciation was making her heart the subject of its regard. A moment before, she had known nothing which she would have sought to hide. Now, as if some secret were hinted to her own consciousness through the medium of another's perception, she was fain to let her eyelids droop beneath Clifford's gaze. A blush, too—the redder, because she strove hard to keep it down—ascended higher and higher, in a tide of fitful progress, until even her brow was all suffused with it.   (p. 220)

"It is enough" Clifford tells her. "Girlhood has passed into womanhood; the bud is a bloom!" Love has turned the girl Phoebe into a woman. She will also have occasion at another point in the novel to remember the explanation of "joy at being in love" which Holgrave ended: "when the truth becomes clear to you, then think of this moonlight scene." Later, when the artist has declared his love for her and asks "Do you love me, Phoebe?" (p. 307), she—again "letting her eyes droop"—will answer "You look into my heart . . . You know I love you!"

In Chapter xiv of Hawthorne's novel love kindled between Holgrave and Phoebe. Though Holgrave had the first inkling of what was happening, Phoebe is soon acknowledging their love with a blush at its realization. Holgrave, more deliberate, will require a final impetus to move him to full commitment. Just before the artist declares his love to Phoebe in Chapter xx, Hawthorne tells us: "These influences [a result of their secret union in the knowledge of Judge Pyncheon's death] hastened the development of emotions, that might not otherwise have flowered so soon. Possibly, indeed, it had been Holgrave's purpose to let them die in their undeveloped germs" (p. 305). The daguerreotypist, however, rejects this possibility as he had refused the opportunity to entrance Phoebe. As he spoke then of the "joy at being in love" he speaks now of a "joy . . . that has made this the only point of life worth living for" (p. 306).

As Chapter xiv ends, Hawthorne's love story is ready for his last step—the mutual declaration of love—and this takes place at the very next meeting of the pair. But Phoebe becomes aware of her state during leave-taking; before she returns the darker side of Hawthorne's plot will have brought Judge Pyncheon to the House of Seven Gables for a famous sit-in.

In meeting the second objection cited at the beginning of this paper I have sought to demonstrate that Hawthorne's conclusion to *The House of the Seven Gables* follows as a natural consequence from the forces he set in motion earlier in the novel. The couple's love and its mollifying effect on Holgrave is not a *deux ex machina*, an artificial close gratuitously provided by the author. The light and allusive handling of a disarmingly straightforward love interest, coupled with an unfortunate omission in the former standard text, has kept scholars from recognizing the relevance of the middle events of the story; but Hawthorne's ending has manifestly been working itself out since the twelfth chapter.

II

The examination so far given Hawthorne's love story has important implications for the first objection tendered against *The House of the Seven Gables*. For one thing, the action is not episodic, not a succession of tableaux; rather, it is cumulative: Chapter xiv carries forward the possibilities which Chapter xii has established; because of the decision to respect the freedom of her soul which precipitates his love for Phoebe, Holgrave can later, in Chapter xx, be committed by circumstances to declaring his affection for her. The failure of Hawthorne's characters to develop or interact has been the source of judgments that the plot is wooden. But both Holgrave and Phoebe develop, and each affects the other deeply. Clifford, as we have seen, also "interacts" with Phoebe; and she has a brightening effect on him. There has been the further charge that Hawthorne's conversations are expository and not dramatic. But Phoebe and Holgrave fall in love in a conversation scene: the moonlight incident is not represented solely by their talk, but the artist's change of mind on the value of the past is, his realization that love moves them is, and almost all of his effect on Phoebe is. Likewise, in Phoebe's scene with Clifford, his words do not tell us she has fallen in love—Hawthorne himself avoids saying so—but she does change in the course of the conversation. Conversations advance the action, and characters affect each other by them.

The plot will also be considered in my discussion of the theme of the novel and how the ending constitutes a working out of it, but one other matter merits attention here while character development is at issue. Of the five principal persons of the book—Phoebe, Hepzibah, Holgrave, Clifford, and Judge Pyncheon—all but the Judge develop in the course of the story and all but Clifford change substantially. I have already suggested the nature of Phoebe's and Holgrave's transformations. Hepzibah, however, is generally considered a static figure. Waggoner has argued quite plausibly that Hawthorne in writing the novel made her less of a type, more of a person, than was his original plan; though Waggoner does not propose that Hepzibah herself changes. He says instead that it is Hawthorne's "treatment of her" that becomes "more and more sympathetic as the story proceeds." Hepzibah does change, however; she is not "unbending," "inadaptive," and "indomitable" as Roy Male would have it. She not only changes, she grows.

Development of true faith in God is what Hawthorne tells us brings about her transformation. Hepzibah's development is gradual. When we first meet Hepzibah, in the very first paragraph of Chapter ii, we watch her kneel to say her prayers (pp. 30–31). Later on the day we meet her, she twice offers briefer pleas to the Almighty (pp. 49, 55). Because of these facts, Male's important observation about an event later in the novel has probably been misleading. He writes: "their trip [flight from the House] has not been a total failure, for here on the isolated platform, lifting her hands to the dull, gray sky, Hepzibah is able to pray—something she has been unable to do in the house." But Hepzibah has prayed, and prayed in the House.

One Sabbath morning after Phoebe has come to the Pyncheon house, her leaving for church leads Clifford to implore Hepzibah that they go too. Looking into Clifford's face Hepzibah is moved by the desire to go and kneel down among the people. Hawthorne designates this as an important point of realization for her: "she *now* recognized" [italics mine] that she was "scarcely friends with Him above." She is moved to go "kneel down among the people, and be reconciled to God and man at once" (p. 168). Her determination is short-lived, however, for when she and Clifford step across the threshold, "the eye of their Father seemed to be withdrawn." She has come to recognize the haughtiness of her spirit, but, failing to act on this realization, she turns back to find "the whole interior of the house tenfold more dismal" (p. 169).

Later, under the pressure of the Judge's threatened undoing of Clifford, Hepzibah will again try to pray: "and [she] strove hard to send up a prayer through the dense, gray pavement of clouds. Those mists had gathered, as if to symbolize a great, brooding mass of human trouble, doubt, confusion, and chill indifference, between earth and the better regions. *Her faith was too weak*; the prayer too heavy to be thus uplifted. It fell back, a lump of lead, upon her heart" (p. 245, italics mine). She tries to pray, but her trust in God is not enough to overcome her doubts—doubts, perhaps, about the very possibility of a solution.

Not until after Judge Pyncheon's death is she able to pray. Befuddled, she at first follows Clifford without a will of her own (pp. 250–251). At the end of "The Flight of Two Owls," however, Clifford is no longer able to guide them: "You must take the lead now, Hepzibah!" (p. 266). Again she has nowhere to turn, again she tries to pray, and this time her faith is enough:

> She knelt down upon the platform where they were standing, and lifted her clasped hands to the sky. *The dull, gray weight of clouds made it invisible; but it was no hour for disbelief;*—no juncture this, to question that there was a sky above, and an Almighty Father looking down from it!
> "Oh, God!"—ejaculated poor, gaunt Hepzibah—then paused for a moment, to consider what her prayer should be— "Oh, God—our Father—are we not thy children? Have mercy on us!"
> (pp. 266–267, italics mine)

Despite the clouds of doubt, it is no time for "disbelief." Hepzibah can trust God enough to pray to him despite her fears and with knowledge of her unworthiness. This time her prayer is heard: Hepzibah and Clifford return to a House of Seven Gables where two lovers have just resolved a hereditary enmity.

Like Holgrave, Phoebe, and even Clifford, Hepzibah changes for the better in *The House of the Seven Gables*. When we first meet her brother he has been demented by thirty years imprisonment; but Hawthorne tells us that had Clifford's exquisite taste been able to develop unhampered, it might have "completely eaten out . . . his affections." For this reason Clifford's "black calamity may . . .

have had a redeeming drop of mercy, at the bottom" (p. 112). Jaffrey's death brightened Clifford's wits enough to make him leader of "The Flight of Two Owls." In the closing chapter we find that despite a subsiding of his exhilaration, the good effect will be lasting: "The Shock of Judge Pyncheon's death had a permanently invigorating and ultimately beneficial effect on Clifford" (p. 313). The novel's main characters are not static.

III

The conclusion of Hawthorne's novel may follow naturally from the characters and their actions, but what of the author-narrator's comments on the action? The author at several points appears to belie his own plot. Matthiessen has said: "[The conclusion] is quite out of keeping with Hawthorne's seemingly deliberate answer in his preface.... For Hawthorne said there that his book might illustrate the truth 'that the wrong-doing of one generation lives into the successive ones, and, divesting itself of every temporary advantage, becomes a pure and uncontrollable mischief.' That unrelenting strain was still at the fore in his final reflections." Hawthorne has told us the moral of his story in the Preface, but it does not seem to fit. According to the author's theme, wrong-doing lives on through consecutive generations, deepening as it goes. If this is the theme of *The House of the Seven Gables*, how can Phoebe and Holgrave, Pyncheon and Maule be reconciled to each other? If this be the moral, how can the progeny of the original Pyncheon malefactor escape his curse?

These knotty questions have generally yielded answers fully satisfactory to no one. It has been maintained, for example, that Hawthorne overlooked disparities of this sort in concluding the novel. When these questions seemed to necessitate considering either the apparent moral or the outcome of the novel spurious, the book's conclusion has usually suffered by the choice. Hoeltje's position, however, is an interesting exception on both counts. He suggests that one would "be gullible to accept seriously the supposed moral." Hawthorne proffered that moral "facetiously." Hoeltje maintains instead that "More than anything else ... *The House of the Seven Gables* depicts the assuaging and recreative power of love." Phoebe and Holgrave represent Sophia and Nathaniel Hawthorne's own love story. Hoeltje's proposals are genuinely helpful for a reading of the novel; but I believe Hawthorne meant his moral to be taken seriously. Hawthorne's theme, however, is wholly reconcilable with the denouement of his plot.

Hawthorne's moral is not incompatible with his plot, primarily because the moral itself admits the possibility of escape from hereditary evils. Almost without exception, when Hawthorne's announced theme is quoted, only the first part of the sentence is cited. But the latter half of the sentence entails a rephrasing of the theme by way of amplification:

> Not to be deficient, in this particular, the Author has provided himself with a moral;—the truth, namely, that the wrong-doing of one generation lives into the successive ones, and, divesting itself of every temporary advantage, becomes a pure and uncontrollable mischief;—and he would feel it a singular gratification, if this romance might effectually convince mankind (or, indeed, any one man) of the folly of tumbling down an avalanche of ill-gotten gold, or real estate, on the heads of an unfortunate posterity, thereby to maim and crush them, until the accumulated mass shall be scattered abroad in its original atoms. (p. 2)

The construction and sense of the sentence equates

> tumbling down an avalanche of ill-gotten gold, or real estate, on the heads of an unfortunate posterity, thereby to maim and crush them, until the accumulated mass shall be scattered abroad in its original atoms

with "wrong-doing." With no injury to the meaning, the sentence could read: the moral is that wrong-doing lives on; the author would be gratified if his romance convinced even one man that wrong-doing lives on. Conversely, the moral is that tumbling down ill-gotten gold to posterity is folly; the author would be gratified if his romance convinced even one man that tumbling down ill-gotten gains to posterity is folly.

This fact about Hawthorne's expression of his theme is crucial, because the explication of the moral which the latter half of the sentence provides suggests that the evil a malefactor drew down on his children's heads would *not* be inexorable. The ill-gotten gold or real estate would maim and crush those who inherited it, *"until the accumulated mass shall be scattered abroad in its original atoms."* The inference is quite definite that when the pilfered wealth shall have gotten back to its original owners, the evil of its acquisition will cease to vex those who had been inheriting it.

In terms of Hawthorne's plot, when the House of Seven Gables, dishonestly wrested from the Maules, shall have been returned to them, the curse acquired with its illicit possession will cease to plague the Pyncheons. This possibility afforded by Hawthorne's moral is realized in the novel's outcome.

On the other hand, the first facet of the moral was that the original wrong-doing would become "pure and uncontrollable mischief," and this facet too is borne out in Hawthorne's story. In *The House of the Seven Gables*, the original act of Pyncheon stealing from Maule would become Pyncheon allowing ill to befall Pyncheon—when Gervayse ignored his daughter Alice's call for help in hopes of recovering the title to Maine territory (p. 204). The next step would be Pyncheon injuring Pyncheon by his own agency—first with some inadvertence when Jaffrey allowed Clifford to be blamed for murder (Jaffrey would become heir), and later with full deliberateness when for the sake of alleged riches (useless to him) Judge Jaffrey will have Clifford committed to a mental institution unless Clifford surrenders a secret. Wrong-doing grows into a "pure and uncontrollable mischief," and the offending family wreaks retribution on its own head.

Hawthorne bears out this reading of his moral by several kinds of statements within the novel. The first type of statement reiterates the *possibility* allowed by the moral: the evil *can be* escaped. Matthew Maule, after an unsuccessful attempt to elicit the secret of the Maine land title from the spirit world says: "It will never be allowed . . . The custody of this secret, that would so enrich his heirs, makes part of your grandfather's *retribution*. He must choke with it, until it is no longer of any value. And keep you the House of the Seven Gables! It is too dear bought an inheritance, and too heavy, with the curse upon it, to be shifted *yet awhile* from the Colonel's posterity" (p. 207, italics mine). The curse is too heavy now for the House to pass from Pyncheon hands, but apparently the curse may be lighter "awhile" in the future, when the Pyncheons will be able to give up the House. Presumably their "retribution" is helping them to atone.

The older Matthew Maule of Holgrave's story was said to haunt the House of Seven Gables offering the alternative that ground-rent be paid or the House given up, "else he, the ghostly creditor, would have his finger in all the affairs of the Pyncheons, and make everything go wrong with them, though it should be a thousand years after his death" (p. 189). *If* he does *not* get ground-rent or the House, he will haunt the Pyncheons. As we have seen, he was not willing to accept the House in exchange just yet, for he preferred to keep the title to the Pyncheon territories hidden until it would be no longer valuable to them. However, he, his grandson, and Holgrave telling the story indicate that the curse was not ineluctable. Their method for putting an end to the ill fortune that haunts the Pyncheons agrees exactly with Hawthorne's moral: the evil will cease to be inherited when the dishonest wealth is returned to the family from which it was originally taken. Gervayse Pyncheon's willingness to give up the House was ineffectual both because he would do so only as part of a bargain extremely profitable to himself, and because for the sake of this bargain he violated his own daughter in breaking a promise to halt the proceedings with Matthew Maule at her "slightest wish" (p. 202).

One other example of this type of statement—suggesting possibilities for escaping an inheritance of "wrong-doing"—is worth noting. Hawthorne himself, closing the chapter which introduced Hepzibah, calls his tale not a story of the inevitable consequences of sin, but a "history of *retribution* for the sin of long ago" (p. 41, italics mine). The author himself, very early in the novel, makes it clear that some kind of atonement is possible.

If atonement is possible, the heritage of evil will have an end. Besides providing references which corroborate the *possibility* of atonement, Hawthorne works into his novel predictions, as well as a description of a landscape, which adumbrate and identify the curse's *termination*. Holgrave explains to Phoebe in Chapter xiv his "conviction . . . that the end draws nigh" in "the drama which, for almost two hundred years, has been dragging its slow length over the ground, where you and I now tread" (pp. 216–217). Later Holgrave will say that he made his way into the part of the House where the Judge sat dead because of "an indefinite sense of some catastrophe, or *consummation*" (p. 303, italics mine). Hawthorne had already used the same word to describe Alice's posies on the morning after the Judge's death: they "seemed, as it were, a mystic expression that something within the house was consummated" (p. 286). Pyncheon retribution reached its peak when the family became its own victim. Judge Jaffrey died while carrying out an action that would have been the "utter ruin" (p. 242) or death (pp. 242–243) of Clifford.

Hawthorne has pointed up the possibility of escaping the curse and confronted us with the fact of consummation in the two-century-old drama, but he goes further. He depicts the House of Seven Gables the morning after the Judge's death as a renewed world. Alice's posies "were flaunting in rich beauty and full bloom" (p. 286), but, more extraordinary, "Every object was agreeable, whether to be gazed at in the breadth, or examined more minutely" (p. 284). The House itself was altered: "there was really an inviting aspect over the venerable edifice, conveying an idea that its history must be a decorous and happy one" (p. 285). Though in one sense explicable—they assure us that the consummation has been beneficial—these changes are in another sense a puzzle. They follow the Judge's death in pursuit of Clifford and are evidence that retribution has been effected. But the results seem disproportionate to the cause; the intended victimizing of Clifford was culpable, and Clifford's actions were not especially meritorious. The family turning against itself may somehow have allowed the curse to pass, but it does not seem to have provided any reason for the House and its environs to be restored to pristine freshness. The gloom might have left the House, but why would it look happy? The love of Phoebe and Holgrave would have been a plausible agent of transformation earlier and would be later, but is not at this point. How are the changes to be accounted for?

The answer, I think, lies not with the Judge's death, except insofar as that may have weakened or helped eliminate the curse. The agency behind the transformations is the mercy of God. Hawthorne playfully allows the inference that God is the agent when he says the House "really" looked as if it had a happy history. For that description seems feasible only in light of his earlier statement that "God is the sole worker of realities" (p. 180). Such evidence is hardly conclusive of course; much more to the point is Hawthorne's description of dawn in the room where the Judge's dead body sat: "Blessed, blessed radiance! The day-beam—even what little of it finds its way into this always dusky parlour— seems part of the universal benediction, annulling evil, and rendering all goodness possible, and happiness attainable. . . . This new day . . . God has smiled upon, and blessed, and given to mankind" (p. 282). Why has God chosen to extend "universal benediction" now? The mercy of God can always be explained as inexplicable, but Hawthorne has given us a better account of its workings within his story. The Judge's death brought to a close the Pyncheon retribution, but Hepzibah had gone on to reach a consummation in personal development. At the end of her flight with Clifford, kneeling on a platform, with hands raised to the sky she had asked

"Oh, God—our Father . . . Have mercy on us!" Her prayer had been heard.

Hawthorne indicates that the hand of God is working in other matters of his story; the Almighty, for example, prevented the *renewal* of the Pyncheon evil. When the Judge forced Hepzibah to admit him to the House so he could question Clifford, she accused him of sacrificing Clifford for his own material gain just as an earlier Pyncheon had sacrificed a Maule. Several of her words echo Hawthorne's statement of the moral of the story in his Preface: "You are but doing over again, in another shape, what your ancestor before you did, and sending down to your posterity the curse inherited from him!" (p. 237). Jaffrey thinks the notion preposterous (though his reply—"Talk sense, Hepzibah, for Heaven's sake"—turns out to be ironic), and Hepzibah, still trying to penetrate his imperviousness, predicts "God will not let you do the thing you meditate!" (p. 237). Left by the Judge's terms with no choice but to let him see her brother, Hepzibah warns: "Be merciful in your dealings with him!—be far more merciful than your heart bids you be!—for God is looking at you, Jaffrey Pyncheon!" (p. 238). At this point it is evident that Hepzibah believes a watchful heaven is mindful of Clifford's plight.

As the old woman leaves to fetch Clifford, however, she is brooding on her family's "dreary past" and comes to feel with foreboding that her cousin, her brother, and she are on the verge of the grimmest event in the House's history, not just a redoing of old wrong, something worse. "Hepzibah now felt as if the Judge, and Clifford, and herself—they three together—were on the point of adding another incident to the annals of the house, with a bolder relief of wrong and sorrow, which would cause it to stand out from all the rest" (pp. 240–241). This, presumably, because the family was turned against itself. Hawthorne does say at this point that "grief of the passing moment" has "a character of climax, which it is destined to lose"; however, he adds, "But Hepzibah could not rid herself of the sense of something unprecedented, at that instant passing, and soon to be accomplished" (p. 241). So her feeling is perhaps not to be considered merely an effect of "the passing moment."

She tries to divert her own attention from its cause of despondency, and eventually seeks the help of the daguerreotypist, who is not in his rooms. Hepzibah sees herself as justifiably friendless, and, lifting her eyes, she tries to pray. As we have already seen, her prayer was not successful this time. But the full explanation of its failure and Hawthorne's dissenting comment are especially worth noting. Hepzibah's prayer "fell back, a lump of lead, upon her heart. It smote her with the wretched conviction, that Providence intermeddled not in these petty wrongs of one individual to his fellow, nor had any balm for these little agonies of a solitary soul, but shed its justice, and its mercy, in a broad, sunlike sweep, over half the universe at once. Its vastness made it nothing" (p. 245). Moments before, Hepzibah had thought that God would not let the Judge renew the curse on the heads of the Pyncheons, that Providence was watching over Clifford. Now, however, she feels that, exactly because He is all mighty, God would not interfere in the daily affairs of individual men.

Hawthorne in no uncertain terms disagrees: "But Hepzibah did not see, that, just as there comes a warm sunbeam into every cottage-window, so comes a love-beam of God's care and pity for every separate need." This is, I believe, the point in *The House of the Seven Gables* where Hawthorne most explicitly connects Providence with his plot. Here, also, God's love-beam is likened to a sunbeam; later the sunbeam is called "Blessed, blessed radiance! The day-beam . . . part of the universal benediction, annulling evil, and rendering all goodness possible, and happiness attainable" (p. 282). By name as well as by action, Phoebe is a sunchild. Holgrave has told her "Providence sent you hither to help" (p. 217).

Hepzibah had warned the Judge "God will not let you do the thing you meditate." Because the Judge was unrelenting, it did take an act of Providence, grim and merciful both, to keep him from a new low in Pyncheon malfeasance. To Holgrave later, Jaffrey's death "so like that former one, yet attended by none of those suspicious circumstances, seems the stroke of God upon him, at once a punishment for his wickedness, and making plain the innocence of Clifford" (p. 304). Judge Pyncheon, the man of affairs, had ignored his old maid cousin's unwittingly prophetical warning.

In the person of Phoebe, the regenerative power of love and the redeeming force of God's mercy minister together. But Hawthorne also speaks in broad terms about the power of love to change things for the better. Chapter xi offers by itself strong evidence that Hawthorne did not mean in his Preface to propose that the wages of sin are both inheritable and ineluctable. When an organ-grinder takes up his stand before the arched window where Phoebe and Clifford watch, they see a show in which "at the same turning of a crank" various figures engage in their appropriate activity. A cobbler works on a shoe, a miser counts his gold, a scholar opens a book and reads. "Yes; and moved by the self-same impulse, a lover saluted his mistress on her lips!" (p. 163). However, "the most remarkable aspect of the affair was, that, at the cessation of the music, everybody was petrified at once . . . into a dead torpor. . . . All were precisely in the same condition as before they made themselves so ridiculous by their haste to toil, to enjoy, to accumulate gold, and to become wise." Hawthorne conjectures as to the meaning of such a show: Perhaps it is meant to signify "that we mortals . . . in spite of our ridiculous activity, bring nothing finally to pass." Examining this "moral," the author considers that the lover would therefore have been "none the happier for the maiden's granted kiss!" But "rather than swallow this last too acrid ingredient," Hawthorne "reject[s] the whole moral of the show." The idea that even love "bring[s] nothing finally to pass" is enough for him to reject the supposed theme. Extended, this means he rejects the thought that even love is helpless when a family is racked by the long possession of ill-gotten gain.

In the final chapter of his romance, Hawthorne utters a statement which, while not so often quoted as the moral of his Preface, has likewise seemed to confute the movement of his story. He is explaining what will be the circumstances of Clifford's life after the Judge's death: "It was now far too late in Clifford's life for the good opinion of society to be worth the trouble and anguish of a formal vindication" (p. 313). The "calm of forgetfulness" will be a greater kindness to Clifford than the exoneration which his townspeople would have been "ready enough" to extend him. "After such wrong as he had suffered, there is no reparation," Hawthorne tells us, and continues with the sentence that has proved almost as troubling as the one in the Preface: "It is a truth (and it would be a very sad one, but for the higher hopes which it suggests) that no great mistake, whether acted or endured, in our mortal sphere, is ever really set right" (p. 313).

Matthiessen has called this the "unrelenting strain . . . still at the fore in [Hawthorne's] final reflections." The novelist seems to have summoned forth again the spectre of inescapable consequences to sin. However, this authorial observation no more runs counter to the movement of Hawthorne's plot than did the sentence in his Preface. The present passage does not mean that the chain of evil consequences to sin is irrefragable, does not mean, in other words, that Phoebe and Holgrave inherit necessarily tainted money and their subsequent years together will be ones of moral decay. In fact, the topic of sin is not raised by the passage in question at all. Hawthorne makes the statement in reference to Clifford's condition: the townspeople who had wrongly sentenced him to prison, though they might exculpate him, could never restore what they had taken from him—thirty years of his life. Hawthorne had not previously suggested and does not here propose that the townsmen sinned in sentencing Clifford, or even that they are culpable. It was Jaffrey's withholding of evidence that produced the mistrial. Thus, in its immediate context, Hawthorne's maxim does not purport to be a reflection on the consequences of an evil act.

"No great mistake, whether acted or endured, in our mortal sphere, is ever really set right." The statement refers *primarily* to the *victim* of a great mistake, rather than to its perpetrators. Hawthorne does say "whether *acted* or endured," but he means, I think, to indicate that the persons responsible for some great injustice have as little power to undo it as the one who suffered from it. The focus is still on the victim and the peculiar difficulties of making restitution to him. Hawthorne's meaning is that no one who suffers great wrong can receive full recompense in this world, either from those who wronged him, or by his own efforts.

Subsequent sentences bear out this reading, for Hawthorne refines and clarifies his generalization in the remarks which follow it. The next sentence is: "Time, the continual vicissitude of circumstances, and the invariable inopportunity of death, render it [really setting great mistakes right] impossible." If the preceding sentence had meant that a misdeed has an irreparable effect on its doer and his progeny as well as on the person who sustained the injury, different agents of continuation would have been named. A world in which one could not escape the effects of the sins of his father would, morally, be timeless. Hawthorne in saying that time, change, and death prevent the undoing of a great mistake is saying that all time is not one time. A person is not inextricably bound by what his foregenitors did. Holgrave did not take the opportunity to gain control over Phoebe even though his ancestor Matthew Maule had attained influence over Alice Pyncheon's soul.

The next sentences are likewise intelligible as statements about undoing harm wrongly afflicted rather than as cautions about the hopelessness of avoiding hereditary effects of sin: "If, after long lapse of years, the right seems to be in our power, we find no niche to set it in. The better remedy is for the sufferer to pass on, and leave what he once thought his irreparable ruin far behind him." The first of these sentences discusses an alternative for those who had "acted" a great mistake, the second offers advice to those who have "endured" one. The first sentence is not applicable to a person seeking to remove the guilt for sin—*that* right never seems to be in our power—though it does apply to a person trying to make up for an injury he once did. Moreover, the second statement advocates something like forgetfulness—strange advice to a person worried about the taint his own or his ancestors' wrongs have left him; humane advice, however, to someone whose reputation and position may be irretrievably and unjustly lost. Hawthorne has just recommended the "calm of forgetfulness" for Clifford.

The statement we have been examining from the last chapter does not conflict with Hawthorne's story; it is a more general amplification of a remark which preceded it: "After such wrong as he had suffered, there is no reparation." Clifford would never be fully restored, but the jury that imprisoned him, and the children of the men who served on it, were not blighted because of their action. A world in which the wrong deliberately or inadvertently done by one's ancestors leaves bleaker hope for oneself would be a constantly darkening world. The world of *The House of the Seven Gables* is optimistic, though Hawthorne's is a careful optimism. Describing "The Daguerreotypist" he had said: "He had that sense, or inward prophecy—which a young man had better never have been born, than not to have, and a mature man had better die at once, than utterly to relinquish—that we are not doomed to creep on forever in the old, bad way, but that, this very now, there are the harbingers abroad of a golden era, to be accomplished in his own lifetime" (p. 179). Hawthorne's thinking a prophetic sense of this kind so necessary suggests what his own view may be. He does not leave us with mere conjecture, however, for in further describing the artist Holgrave he makes his own view explicit. The daguerreotypist, he tells us, was wrong "in supposing that this age, more than any past or future one, is destined to see the tattered garments of Antiquity exchanged for a new suit, instead of gradually renewing themselves by patchwork; in applying his own little lifespan as the measure of an interminable achievement; and, more than all, in fancying that it mattered anything to the great end in view, whether he himself should contend for it or against it" (p. 180). Holgrave might overestimate his own place in the brightening history of mankind, but that human history is brightening, Hawthorne fully agrees: "As to the main point —may we never live to doubt it!—as to the better centuries that are coming, the artist was surely right."

4. Divergent Conclusions

D. H. Lawrence

Nothing Compared to "The Scarlet Letter"

Hawthorne's other books are nothing compared to *The Scarlet Letter*.

But there are good parables, and wonderful dark glimpses of early Puritan America, in *Twice Told Tales*.

The House of the Seven Gables has "atmosphere". The passing of the old order of the proud, bearded, black-browed Father: an order which is slowly ousted from life, and lingeringly haunts the old dark places. But comes a new generation to sweep out even the ghosts, with these new vacuum cleaners. No ghost could stand up against a vacuum cleaner.

The new generation is having no ghosts or cobwebs. It is setting up in the photography line, and is just going to make a sound financial thing out of it. For this purpose all old hates and old glooms, that belong to the antique order of Haughty Fathers, all these are swept up in the vacuum cleaner, and the vendetta-born

---

From *Studies in Classic American Literature* by D. H. Lawrence. Copyright 1923, renewed 1951 by Frieda Lawrence. Reprinted by permission of The Viking Press, Inc.

young couple effect a perfect understanding under the black cloth of a camera and prosperity. *Vivat Industria!*

Oh, Nathaniel, you savage ironist! Ugh, how you'd have *hated* it if you'd had nothing but the prosperous, "dear" young couple to write about! If you'd lived to the day when America was nothing but a Main Street.

The Dark Old Fathers.

The Beloved Wishy-Washy Sons.

The Photography Business.

? ? ?

T. S. Eliot

Hawthorne's Best Novel After All

Compare, with anything that any English contemporary could do, the situation which Hawthorne sets up in the relation of Dimmesdale and Chillingworth. Judge Pyncheon and Clifford, Hepzibah and Phoebe, are similarly achieved by their relation to each other; Clifford, for one, being simply the intersection of a relation to three other characters. The only dimension in which Hawthorne could expand was the past, his present being so narrowly barren. It is a great pity, with his remarkable gift of observation, that the present did not offer him more to observe. But he is the one English-writing predecessor of James whose characters are *aware* of each other, the one whose novels were in any deep sense a criticism of even a slight civilization; and here is something more definite and closer than any derivation we can trace from Richardson or Marivaux.

. . .

Reprinted from "The Hawthorne Aspect," *Little Review,* vol. V, pp. 51. 53 (August 1918) by permission of Mrs E. V. Eliot and Faber and Faber Ltd.

Compare the book [*The Sense of the Past*] with *The House of the Seven Gables* (Hawthorne's best novel after all); the situation, the "shrinkage and extinction of a family" is rather more complex, on the surface, than James's with (so far as the book was done) fewer character-relations.